CAN WE RUN WITH YOU, GRANDFATHER?

CAN WE RUN WITH YOU, GRANDFATHER?

SEVEN CONTINENTS:
SEVEN DECADES

DOUG RICHARDS

A2 Yeoman Gate
Yeoman Way
Worthing
Sussex
BN13 3QZ
www.pitchpublishing.co.uk
info@pitchpublishing.co.uk

© 2018, Doug Richards

ISBN 978-1-78531-445-2

Typesetting and origination by Pitch Publishing
Printed and bound in the UK by TJ International Ltd

Contents

Dedication

To Mum and Dad.
Thank you – it's all down to you both. I wish
you had been there to see the fun that I have
had.

Foreword by the author

I feel so privileged to have enjoyed the life I have led, but it hasn't always been easy and I have had a lot of support on the way from family and friends. To list them all would be an impossible task, so if your name doesn't appear below and you have been one of those who have backed me on my journey, then thank you from the bottom of my heart.

To my daughter, Angela, and son, Chris – I am so proud of you both and the caring people you have grown into. Thank you for your unquestioning and never-ending support of my crazy ventures. May you live long and happy lives with your brilliant spouses, Ben and Lynne, and find some time for some spectacular adventures of your own.

To my two delightful grand-daughters, Holly and Josie. It has been such a joy to run with you both and I hope you too can find time in your busy future lives for some adventures of your own. I know you both love animals and nature.

To my sister Lin, a marathon runner in her time, who maybe has lapsed a little. I know you are always supportive of me darling and you're always in my thoughts when I am away in faraway places.

To my brother Dave and his wife Allie; I was never quite able to convince you to take up this running lark but I know you are both 100% behind me, both during my adventures and with the writing and speaking career that has grown out of it. I forgive you, Dave, for trying to destroy my reputation at my

70th birthday party, by reading excerpts from the logbooks of our adolescent camping trips!

The wonderful friends I have made from running, from both at home and around the world, are far too numerous to thank individually. Some of you may find your names mentioned in this book but, to each and every one of you, I could not have achieved what I have without you and I hope we meet again soon. I will just mention two very special friends; Julie and Phillipa. We always enjoy a good run or race together but I know that, when life isn't going so smoothly for me, you are always there with your caring friendship and support.

Finally, special thanks to my friend, Sue, from Redditch U3A, who not only convinced me that I had a talent for writing, but has been a constant source of advice since, and has played a major role in the editing of the manuscripts for both this and my previous book.

Chapter 1

From Bhuna to Burma

'And the journey hasn't ended yet.'

These were the words with which I finished my previous book, *Running Hot & Cold*, and as it turned out I wasn't wrong. As before, it was no free-flowing journey through life but the usual mixture of euphoria followed by disappointment, and repeat.

Yes, I am the same ageing pensioner who, as a teenage boy who hated running, jumped on a bus when out of sight of his teachers during a school road run, to conserve his youthful energy. The same young man who believed sport was something you watched with a pint in your hand, rather than something you took part in. Even my token attempts at playing cricket were merely a prelude to the shenanigans in the bar after the match.

But eventually it caught up with me. Struggling to console a crying child because running up a single flight of steps had left me out of breath, I vowed to run a mile the next morning. It hurt; it hurt a lot, but I still felt pleased with myself. If you had grabbed me by my sweaty shoulders that morning and told me what the consequences of that single decision would be, there is no way I would have believed you. But it happened.

I have run during a Siberian winter. I have run along the Great Wall of China. I even ran away from angry elephants in South Africa and covered huge distances in the stifling heat of the Sahara Desert. And, in the immediate aftermath of the 2004 Indian Ocean tsunami, I ran to the summit of that mountainside road in the devastated country of Sri Lanka, where a small child, standing by the roadside with a few of his friends, called out to me, 'Can we run with you, grandfather?'

Of course I said 'yes' and it is the minutes that followed as we ran and sang our way down the other side of the mountain that will forever live in my memory, and which sum up why I love running so much.

So, the journey hadn't ended yet. Now, where were we?

I had just completed a half marathon in Greenland, including a few kilometres on the mile-thick polar ice cap. Now, not many pensioners can claim that. I had also discovered, as a Leader in Running Fitness for England Athletics, the satisfaction of passing on my knowledge and experience to new runners, who were eager to incorporate exercise into their lives, which in this pressured day and age can bring so many challenges. That is something I will return to later. In the meantime, parkrun was becoming an increasingly important part of my life. I'm not looking for sympathy, but it is a fact of life that if you live on your own and retire from work, you are likely to spend an awful lot of time alone unless you make a concerted effort to make sure that doesn't happen. There was no danger of that happening to me when I was surrounded by such an enthusiastic running community.

* * * * *

As we moved into the summer of 2014, another unforgettable life moment was fast approaching; the wedding of my only daughter, Angela. It had come perhaps a few years later than it might have done and Angela had been through a few tough times in her life, but there was no doubt in my mind that now she had found true happiness with Ben. You may recall that it was Ben who graciously allowed Angela to fulfil her safari dream and come to Africa with me shortly after they had moved in together. Indeed, the date they had chosen for their wedding was 21 June, the second anniversary of 'Elephant Day', when Angela, on her sick-bed at the time, endured the sounds of roaring, trumpeting and gunfire that marked the escape of our party of runners from a chasing herd of angry elephants. Angela and Ben had since been blessed with a beautiful daughter, Josie, and were as happy as any family could be. Ever the gentleman, Ben even phoned me on the eve of Valentine's Day to seek my permission to ask Angela to marry him. I couldn't have been happier to give it and had a massive smile on my face when Angela phoned me the following day to ask if I had been keeping secrets from her! The wedding day could not have gone better. A wonderful venue in the shadow of the Sussex Downs and even the sun chose to shine brightly on us all. A proud moment for any father.

* * * * *

One new hobby I had taken up when I initially retired from work in 2011 had been hen-keeping. Not on a commercial scale, of course, but I had a reasonable-sized, enclosed back garden and, not being at all green fingered, I was pretty tolerant of any damage that hens might do to any delicate plants. Korma, Tikka and Bhuna provided many happy memories, not to mention a relentless supply of eggs. Their names in no way reflected their eventual fate and I'm happy to say that they lived a life few chickens get to live. Fruit and vegetables would rain over the garden fence from my neighbours and every Sunday a carrier bag of potato and vegetable peelings would magically appear on my garden gate for consumption during the week. It was difficult, if not impossible, to look out of the kitchen window and not smile at their antics as they scratched around in the garden, pursued rogue magpies after their tit-bits or ganged together to chase any inquisitive cats back over the fence. My own cat, Nougat, very quickly learned to keep her distance and would sprint for the safety of the cat flap when the coast was clear.

One downside, of course, was that hen-keeping was pretty time-consuming with early mornings to let them out of their coop and locking them away at night to keep them safe from foxes. Hens also produce a surprisingly large amount of 'waste material' which, when added to the compost bin, eventually produced a very fine fertiliser. Bhuna, in particular, tended to save up her droppings for one major effort. One of the highlights of any visit from my grand-daughter, Holly, would be the daily 'poo patrol' with bucket and trowel, and the search for the occasional 'Bhuna bombs'.

I was also heavily reliant on the goodwill of my neighbours when I wanted to spend any length of time away from home and this was always forthcoming, particularly from John next door, who sadly is no longer with us. Any absence of more than a single day meant more work than simply topping up food and water containers in order to keep the coop in a hygienic condition.

But all good things come to an end and it's never an easy time when they do. I lost Korma just before Christmas of 2013. She had never really recovered fully from a nasty respiratory infection and then I found her collapsed on the lawn one evening and she died in my arms within minutes. Tikka succumbed to an internal haemorrhage just six months later, but Bhuna seemed to be managing so well as a solo hen; she was always the strongest and most robust of the three.

It was after returning from Angela's fantastic wedding weekend in Sussex that John reported Bhuna hadn't seemed her usual perky self and had spent most of the final day hiding under a bush. Despite a trip to the vet and a course of antibiotics for a mild chest infection, she was never the same again. She ate less and less, even ignoring her favourite treats of tomato, banana or mealworms, and no longer did she have the energy to chase off the magpies. She looked forlorn, struggling to cope with the summer heat, and I knew deep down her journey was run. We returned to the vets for the final time. It was likely that she was in kidney failure; they could do tests to confirm it but there was no treatment at her age. I stroked her black feathers for the final time and bade her a teary farewell, but I knew it was for the best. I couldn't watch her suffer any longer.

I look back on my hen-keeping days with fond memories and console myself with the fact that they all lived a happy life. I would love to have had more but they were a tie and restricted my time away from home. So there were to be no more, but the silver lining of ending this particular chapter was that it gave me a little more freedom, and my running shoes were getting restless again.

* * * * *

Now it was me-time, and a bit of a holiday. Those who know me well know that I'm not a beach, swimming-pool, gin and tonic type of person; for me it's a question of where my running shoes could take me next. With a little more freedom after Bhuna's sad demise, I could look further afield. I would still have to rely on neighbours to look after my cat but at least she was capable of making arrangements for disposing of her own waste material! The dream of seven continents was still at the back of my mind, with South America, Australia and Antarctica still waiting to be ticked off, although the latter still seemed to be a financial impossibility. As far as distance was concerned, the half marathon still seemed to be the best option for my age and ability; long enough to provide a stern test in difficult climatic conditions but not so far as to risk being 'timed out' if the run didn't go according to plan. Dublin, Lisbon and Berlin were all half marathon possibilities but the lure of something a little more exotic was strong. In the end, I settled on a race that would do nothing to advance my seven continents dream but would take me back to the hot and humid conditions I had struggled with in Sri Lanka. I planned to return to Asia, a continent I had grown to love, and signed up with Adventure Marathons again to run the Bagan Temple half marathon in Myanmar, more commonly known to the British as Burma, a country that had been largely closed to Westerners in recent times.

Whenever I consider running in a country that is not really on the tourist trail, my first port of call is to read the advice on the Foreign Office website, and then usually to ignore it and cross my fingers. Although political tensions had eased in Burma since the release of Aung San Suu Kyi, there were still parts of the country that were strictly off limits. Fortunately, our itinerary took us nowhere near those. 'Railway equipment is poorly maintained; fatal crashes occur although they may not always be reported,' the website stated. No problem, as the itinerary was free of any rail travel! 'There are concerns over safety standards of some airlines operating within Burma.' Not so good, as we had three internal flights scheduled. There was a high threat of terrorism and attacks could be indiscriminate, but then you could say that about London, or anywhere else in the world for that matter. The fact is that if I had taken heed of the advice before my trips to Jordan and South Africa, I might never have gone and, as a consequence, missed two fabulous experiences. Nothing in life is without risk and, as the Foreign Office site concluded, as long as you take sensible precautions, most visits are trouble-free. I signed the race entry form, booked my flights and, the next morning, passed on the news to my grand-daughter, Holly, who was staying with me at the time.

We looked at the globe to see where Myanmar was and, as is the way of the world these days, she immediately grabbed her tablet computer and began to research feverishly.

'Grandad, did you know that there are still wild tigers living in Myanmar?' A pause, and then, 'Grandad, some of the world's largest pythons live there.'

There was then a deep intake of breath before she said, 'You do realise that there are elephants living in Myanmar, don't you?' Then, with hands on hips, she delivered the final rebuke.

'Grandad, why do you always have to run in countries where dangerous animals live?'

It was a fair question and, one day, I hope she will understand.

* * * * *

It was also a time to think about a new chapter in my fundraising activities. For some time I had been supporting the Royal Air Force Association, including my runs in Rome, South Africa and Greenland, and now felt the need for a change. This time I chose the Midlands Air Ambulance Charity. Like many, I was stunned to discover that this absolutely vital life-saving service received not a penny of government funding, relying entirely on public donations to keep it operational. Anybody might require its services at any time, from the youngest infant to the oldest pensioner, and the access to immediate skilled medical help combined with a speedy transition to hospital can so often be the difference between life and death. Whether it be a road traffic accident or someone, like myself, with a love of the great outdoors who suddenly finds themselves in difficulties far from help, the helicopter is a lifeline.

* * * * *

There were less than five months between Angela's wedding and the race in Myanmar but it was a period when my running was well on track. From the time I had retired, my monthly mileage had progressively increased and 100-mile-plus months were becoming the norm. In fact, 2014 was to eventually prove to be my best annual mileage ever, even beating the time when I was preparing for the Marathon des Sables. And it wasn't just the total distance I had run that was improving – my pace over the shorter distances was gradually advancing too. Over the course of the year, I was regularly running under 25 minutes for the parkrun 5k and now my personal best was edging towards that elusive 24-minute barrier. Now, I am not one of those people who can run eyeballs-out, week in week out. Don't get me wrong, I have every admiration for those who do but, for me, my parkrun performance often depended on how I felt on my mile-and-a-half warm-up run to the start. If I felt a bit below par, then it would probably end as a steady run, perhaps pacing someone to their target time with a bit of chit-chat along the way. If I felt good, then I may well have gone for it and tried to chip a few seconds off that elusive personal best.

The date 13 September 2014 was a very special day for me – the day I would complete my 100th parkrun and qualify to wear the black milestone '100' T-shirt. I wouldn't be the first of our regular Arrow Valley parkrun community to reach that prestigious target, as others had discovered parkrun elsewhere before I did, but I would be the first who had begun their journey at Arrow Valley, shortly after our event started in the summer of 2012.

I had made a secret pledge to myself beforehand. I would give it my all to try and achieve a personal best on that special day, which at the time stood at 24 minutes and nine seconds. I hadn't told any of my friends for fear of putting myself under too much pressure. Unbeknown to me, one of my colleagues, John, had arranged for our coach, Ernie, to pace him to a personal best on that very day, too. Now John, who had a couple more birthdays under his belt than I did, might be described as one of my parkrun nemeses. The whole ethos of parkrun is that it is a run and not a race – the only person you are competing against is yourself. However, when you run every week, you get to know the people who run at a similar pace to you, and it would take a special type of person who didn't feel at least a bit competitive with those around. To be fair to John, he finished ahead of me far more often than I did of him, but there was always an element of friendly competition between us.

If my memory serves me correctly, it was me who made the faster start but John came past me on the first of the two laps, with Ernie just a couple of yards behind, barking out instructions in his rich Glaswegian accent. It was only then that I realised they were working together and I tried to stay as close to them as I could. I felt good, I felt strong, and on the second lap I moved past them both, although never that far away as I could always hear Ernie's constant urgings. As we entered the final couple of hundred yards, I picked up my pace to what, for me, was a full-on sprint.

'Come on, you can catch him, you can catch him,' shouted Ernie from behind and I could hear John's footsteps gradually getting closer, however hard I tried. John caught me just before the line. In horse-racing parlance, he took it by a short head, although we were both given the time of 23 minutes and 40 seconds, a personal best for us both that has stood to this very day. I had done what I had set out to do on my 100th parkrun, and my joy was as great the following day when I ran a 10k around the lanes and streets of Stratford in under 50 minutes for the first time in 12 years. If ever I was in good enough shape to take on one of my foreign adventures, it was now.

* * * * *

Unlike the build-up to my Greenland trip, when I had been gripped by a bout of anxiety just a couple of weeks before departure, life was good as I packed my bags for the outward journey for Myanmar. Unlike most of my previous long-distance trips, where I had met up with the race organisers and fellow runners in London, Paris or Copenhagen, before flying onwards together as a group, on this occasion I would not meet anyone associated with the race until I reached the hotel in Yangon.

Travelling alone was something I was used to but memory can play funny tricks on you as you get older and I was constantly checking pockets and wallets to make sure I still had everything I needed at each stage of the journey. There was also a slight concern about my entry visa into Myanmar. The traditional approach had been to obtain one in person from the Burmese Embassy in London: yes, the UK Foreign Office still referred to the country as Burma. However, their website informed me that they were trialling a new online procedure and this had the advantage of saving me a trip down to the capital. I filled in the requisite forms and was presented with a document, a pre-visa, which I would be required to present at immigration in Yangon. Rather worryingly, it stated that it did not guarantee me entry into the country. So, I could travel all the way to Myanmar and then be turned back at the border. Perhaps it would have been easier to have the visa stamp safely in my passport after all.

The first leg of the journey was a long flight to Singapore, most of which took place in darkness. The huge A380 aircraft was not too busy and I at least had the luxury of three seats to myself, which made sleeping easier, although I never find this anything but stop-start on a long flight. Between snatches of slumber, I was peering at the little screen on the back of the seat in front that was tracking our journey, and was surprised to see us flying directly over Kabul, albeit at 39,000 feet, at a time when it was far from peaceful on the ground there. Nevertheless, we arrived in Singapore safely and with just a few hours to kill before catching my connecting flight to Yangon, it gave me the opportunity to familiarise myself with Changi Airport as I would have a much longer overnight stay there on my return journey.

The onward morning flight to Yangon was uneventful, and then, it was cross your fingers time as I entered immigration. I joined a long and very slow-moving queue and when I eventually got to the front, presented my passport and 'pre-visa' form to the clerk behind the glass. I was immediately informed I had been in the wrong queue and was directed to a solitary uniformed official, standing by a gate. He took one look at my form, stamped my passport with the visa and opened the gate. I was in! Maybe the online option was the way forward after all.

There was just one more task; we weren't permitted to bring local currency into Myanmar and were advised to bring US dollars. I went to the exchange desk and my handful of dollar bills were instantly transformed into a huge bundle of

Burmese kyat banknotes, far too fat a bundle to comfortably fit into my wallet.

I stepped into the arrivals hall and scanned the faces and held-up placards in the forlorn hope that there might be a representative of the tour company to greet us, but to no avail. Predictably, and almost immediately, I was swamped by offers of help with my bag and transport to the hotel. It can be so easy to get ripped off in situations like this and the secret I had learned was to agree a price before stepping into any vehicle. I soon found a man, speaking perfect English, who was prepared to do the trip for the equivalent of nine pounds, which turned out to be a very good deal given that the journey took us the best part of an hour.

As we set off towards the city in the heat and humidity of the early afternoon, the driver chatted amiably about the reasons for my visit, whilst pointing out landmarks along the way. We very soon reached gridlocked roads; the traffic was horrendous. Apparently this was due to the government subsidising the purchase of cars in the capital in an effort to boost the economy although now, if anything, the traffic standstill was having the opposite effect. As we edged past glorious parklands, the driver would occasionally wind down his window, cough from deep within his stomach and then spit violently on to the road outside, before continuing with his tour guiding. Our party were due to leave Yangon the following morning, leaving me with only one evening to explore the city; clearly nowhere near long enough, but again the driver came to the rescue by informing me that my hotel was very close to the towering Shwedagon Pagoda, and this was a must-see.

As I dragged my heavy suitcase into the lobby of the hotel, I was relieved to see a lone figure in a pale blue T-shirt with 'Adventure Marathon' written on the back. First contact with the race organisers. Thor introduced himself before helping me through the check-in process and then sitting down to outline the programme for the following 24 hours. Apparently, very few of the competitors had arrived thus far, including the person I would be rooming with, an American called Jeffrey. I explained that I wanted to visit the Shwedagon Pagoda and Thor assured me that Yangon was a very safe city to walk around alone, although he did advise against running in the streets, not because of the risk of being mugged, but the fact that you might fall down into one of the many holes in the pavement! Yangon is not renowned for its ability to maintain its public walkways.

I did set out alone for a walk to the Pagoda and, being fairly conspicuous as a tourist with a camera round my neck, was greeted by several locals in a friendly fashion. Some parts of the walk were very pleasant and photogenic, but on some of the side roads people were living in tents in extraordinarily squalid conditions and the stench was quite unbearable. The other instant impression I gained of Yangon was of the number of stray dogs on the streets, often with a family of puppies in tow. They seemed very placid but I wasn't going to approach any of them to find out and I was happy that my rabies jab was up to date. And Thor was not wrong with regard to the pavements. Huge, and I mean huge, holes appeared at regular intervals, often dropping six feet or more into the drains below.

In the end, I settled for taking some external photos of the Pagoda and then returned to the hotel in the hope of meeting more of my running colleagues. Still Jeffrey hadn't arrived but outside the hotel room window was a wonderful view, a beautiful lake with a few fountains spraying up into the air and, it seemed, a footpath all around it, with pairs of monks in their Buddhist tunics wandering at peace. My legs were tense and tight from the long flights and the walk to the Pagoda, and the prospect of a gentle run to ease them was just too tempting. It also meant I could add a run in Yangon to the ever-growing list of places I had run in. I quickly donned my vest and shorts and set out in the early-evening sunshine to the gates of the park. I had run barely 200 yards, when two men, smoking cigarettes, rose from a bench and blocked my path. Was I being mugged? They would be sorely disappointed as I had nothing on me.

'Five US dollars please,' said one.

I held my hands out wide, showing them that I had no money.

'I am sorry,' he replied in a polite manner. 'I'm afraid there is a charge of five US dollars to use our parks. If you want to run, you will have to run in the streets.'

I turned and left. We take it for granted that we can generally use our parks and open spaces without charge but this beautiful location was clearly a revenue stream for the city, or perhaps even for the men themselves.

I did get my run in Yangon. It was only about a mile and the humidity was oppressive. I chose a route that I had walked just an hour or two earlier and, although the light was beginning to fade, I knew exactly where the potholes were, and managed to avoid them.

* * * * *

I ate pasta in the hotel restaurant that evening and, at last, began to meet some of my fellow runners. I was wearing my Petra half marathon T-shirt and race-wear is always a great way to start a conversation amongst runners who haven't met before. After a couple of hours of lively reminiscing, I went back to my room for an early night – we had a 3.50am alarm call the following morning for our flight to Mandalay.

I was lying on my bed when Jeffrey eventually arrived.

'Hello, I'm Jeffrey,' he announced in a strong New York accent. 'You must be Doug.' There was a pause of a few seconds as we looked at each other with an unsaid 'Don't I know you from somewhere' expression on our faces.

Then the penny dropped. Greenland, we'd met in Greenland. We hadn't particularly spent much of that time together, occasionally chatting at mealtimes, but nevertheless, we had met before.

Jeffrey, a few years younger than me, was a New York lawyer. What set him apart on both this, and the Greenland trip, was that he wasn't a runner. He had been a fairly successful athlete in the past but no longer enjoyed it. He did, however, enjoy travel to unusual locations and loved the positive attitude to life that most runners have. Therefore, he tended to book his holidays with running travel companies, and then plan his own excursions while the rest of us were out running. On this trip, he had three friends travelling with him, only one of whom would be taking part in the race. He apologised in advance to me in case my sleep was disturbed as he liked to get up very early in the morning, and he also said he would spend a long time in the bathroom readying himself for the day ahead. We would not spend a lot of time together over the course of the holiday, but when we did, the conversation was always lively.

The alarm call came as scheduled. Jeffrey had been up since before 3am. We ate a brief breakfast before a coach took us to the airport for our 6am flight to Mandalay. It was on the coach that we first met our local guide, Sun Sun. She was a mother with a family of her own but would be giving up a week of her time to make sure we were as informed about our visit as possible. What Sun Sun didn't know about the history, culture, practices and politics of Myanmar wasn't worth knowing. She was absolutely superb.

* * * * *

After the 90-minute flight to Mandalay, we boarded our coach for a sightseeing tour of the surrounding area. Now was really a chance to get to know some of our fellow runners, none of whom I'd met before but, as is usually the case on these trips, they came from all corners of the planet. On the coach, I sat next to Otto, who was a few years younger than me and a German general practitioner with a great sense of humour. We immediately bonded and would develop a lasting friendship.

First a visit to the U Bein bridge, whose history Sun Sun regaled us with. Built of teak in 1782, it spanned 1.2 kilometres across the Taungthaman Lake, making it the longest wooden bridge in the world. We walked along its seemingly fragile structure. In the waters below, colourful canoe-like boats were being punted along by their pilot standing at the rear, the remaining occupants seated and sheltering from the sun beneath their parasols. Fishermen and fisherwomen were everywhere; not just those on the shoreline of the lake casting their nets into the waters, but the lake was shallow enough to allow men and women in their brightly coloured costumes to wade out several metres from the shoreline, rod in hand, to fish for their evening meal. On a low, wooden jetty, seemingly floating on the lake's surface, two young women were bathing and washing their hair using buckets and pans. Running water was a luxury in these parts.

We moved on to the Mahagandayon Monastery, home to over a thousand Buddhist monks. It was their lunchtime and they queued patiently, black-lacquered bowl in hand and a brightly coloured napkin over their left wrist. Young and old, the senior monks in their purple tunics, the young boy novices in white. In the streets surrounding the monastery, young families sat at the kerbside, begging for offerings from the clearly more affluent visitors. The children, and many of the young women's faces, were smeared with thanaka paste, a feature of the culture of Myanmar; a cosmetic product accentuating their facial features, but also offering protection from the sun, and a sight we would get used to in the days to come. New buildings were still being erected at the monastery, the men working feverishly, but not very effectively, haphazardly applying mortar to the bricks in the hot sun, while women, canvas hats covering their hair, would carry eight bricks at a time, balanced on their heads, to the bricklayers.

We moved on again. A woodcarving and textile workshop, with skilled workers using not only their hands but also their feet; just amazing. Next, the Mahamuni Buddha Temple, housing the Mahamuni Buddha Image, cast in bronze and weighing no less than six and a half tons. As kneeling monks recited from the scriptures, male devotees applied gold leaves to the face of the Buddha image. Only males were permitted to enter the front enclosure surrounding the image; a golden entry gate carrying a red sign stated 'Ladies are not allowed to enter'.

The relentless itinerary was briefly interrupted by a pause for lunch and a chance to get to know some more of our party; Alma, an emergency room medic from the US, and her friend Jill, who worked in the world of finance. At the time, *Running Hot & Cold* was just six weeks away from being published as an e-book and I wasted no opportunity to talk about the running adventures I had had. Being an author was a whole new adventure for me and I had no idea at the time where it would lead.

Our final visit of a busy day was to the carved wooden Golden Palace Monastery on the outskirts of Mandalay. Now this was absolutely extraordinary. The whole monastery was made of wood and the fine detail on the carvings was exquisite. To be honest, it is difficult to put into words just how intricate this building was, not only on the grand scale with its three-tiered wooden roof thronged with thousands of individually carved figurines, but also the detail on the carvings that adorned the wooden walls of the temple. My mind wandered back to the Mogao caves in China and, of course, to the Terracotta Army – the skills of the craftsmen in both ancient, and in rather more recent historical times, was extraordinary.

We now journeyed to our home for the night, the beautiful Sedona Hotel in Mandalay, its entrance bisecting two large pools of blue water alive with hundreds of Koi. There was such a contrast between the hustle and bustle of Yangon, and the relative tranquillity of Mandalay, yet this was nothing compared to the contrasts we would soon be seeing in the less affluent areas of Myanmar.

After booking into our splendid hotel, we spent a relaxing hour chatting by the large outdoor swimming pool in the warm afternoon sunshine before the idea was mooted that some of us might want to go for a run. It was not universally accepted; for many the attractions of the pool's warm, blue waters were just too great and there would be time for running later. In the end, just four of us met to go for the run; myself, Otto and a Swedish husband and wife, Henrik and Malin. Directly opposite our hotel was the old Palace of Mandalay, largely hidden by an imposing wall and surrounded by a very wide moat. The wall formed an almost exact square, each side being a little under a mile and a half long and we set off together to run around the whole perimeter. It was to be one of those magical runs – a beautiful setting in a far, far away city with great people for company. We shared our life stories; Henrik and Malin were both engineers and had a young family at home. Like me, Otto was divorced but had two sons. Henrik was a far faster runner than the rest of us but we stayed together, taking care not to trip on the sometimes uneven surface. The local people would look at us in disbelief – social running was obviously not widely practised in Mandalay – but a cheery retort of that all-purpose greeting in Myanmar, 'mingalaba', would bring a wide grin to their faces before they responded with the same and waved us on. Ahead, huge flocks of pigeons would gather across the entire pathway, not moving out of our way until the very last second when we would be engulfed in a whirlwind of feathers and dust.

As we turned south to run the final leg of the square, the sun was setting in the west. I did not have a camera with me to record that view, but it will be forever imprinted on my mind. The sky was a collage of reds, oranges, purples and crimsons; the waters of the moat carried the reflection, almost appearing to be on fire, and in between the palace buildings glowed in the colours of the sunset. It was a perfect run.

* * * * *

The following morning we boarded a wooden boat for a trip up the Ayeyarwady River to Mingun, a dolphin protection area, although we were not fortunate enough to see any. The moorings were chaotic, with large boats being moored ten abreast and those nearest the shore seemingly having no chance of getting out on to the river. We boarded from a muddy bank along a 15-foot-long narrow plank, barely a foot wide. Two crew members, a young man and young girl, her cheeks painted with thanaka, held a long wooden pole to one side for us to grasp as we took it in turns to walk the plank. Soon we were on our way, our boat mercilessly barging other craft out of the way to create a channel to the wide river. Traffic was busy: houseboats and low-slung fishing vessels zig-zagged around in the shallow waters to avoid the sandbanks that, from time to time, penetrated the surface of the river. Of course, we were now a captive audience and very soon the crew had a range of local craftware out on display, urging us to purchase.

In time we arrived at Mingun, home of the monumental Unfinished Pagoda, built on the orders of King Bodawpaya but never finished as an astrologer had claimed that the king would die were it to be completed. The steep, sand-coloured outer walls were scarred by huge cracks caused by earthquakes over many centuries.

Once again, disembarking was a tricky procedure; there was no jetty as such, just a steep, slippery muddy bank to negotiate with the aid of the narrow plank. Once ashore, and perhaps for the first time, we encountered the true poverty that is the real Myanmar, and yet the people were so friendly and welcoming, if not a little over-zealous in trying to part us from our money with a rich and colourful variety of offerings of food, clothing and crafts. We visited the 90-ton Mingun Bell, the second largest functioning bell in the world, and then the spectacular Myatheindan Pagoda, a gleaming, white castle-like structure capped with a white dome and a golden tower. Outside, taxis were waiting to ferry us back to our boat but these were no motorised vehicles; two-wheeled wooden carts with a knotted, wicker roof and drawn by two cattle. Most of us walked but a few took on the challenge.

We clambered, or were hauled, aboard and then came one of those moments that classically illustrated the contrast in culture between our two societies. Our pilot started the engine and pulled away before his crew had finished untying us from another vessel we were tethered to. A splintering of wood as a chunk of handrail on the other boat was torn off and fell into the water below. There were no insurance details to be exchanged, just a shrug between the two skippers and then as we moved off, the other pilot leant out of his boat to retrieve the broken pieces and set about fixing them.

There were further visits that day to gold-leaf and textile workshops and once again the levels of craftsmanship were eye-opening. One of the early stages of making the gold leaf was to hammer flat the small pieces of gold, each sandwiched between layers of fabric. Four young men stood side by side, naked to the waist, and slammed heavy, long-handled hammers from over their heads down on to the anvils to which the packages of gold and fabric were attached. It was a strictly choreographed process – bang, bang, bang, bang – pause – bang, bang, bang, bang – pause – and the sweat poured off them as they toiled.

But now it was time to move on from our brief but enticing visit to Mandalay to our final destination, where the true purpose of our visit, the running, would take place. The area around Bagan in central Myanmar is dominated by over 2,000 Buddhist stupas, pagodas and temples, dating back almost a thousand years, and it would be in this extraordinary landscape that we would run our race. We boarded a short flight to Bagan, arriving at our new hotel in darkness, so unaware of the beautiful temples and primitive villages that surrounded us as we ate dinner that evening by the pool in the moonlight.

Chapter 2

A dog called Doug

Pre-race day is not one on which you would want to spend a lot of time on your feet. I clearly remember the grumbles from some of the more elite runners before the race in Petra, Jordan, as we spent hours in the hot, baking sunshine exploring what is an absolutely unique and fascinating city at any other time. Our schedule in Myanmar was somewhat more relaxed, although again the sunshine and humidity had their own draining effect.

I was fast becoming a hardened fan of such a beautiful, yet secretive country. I don't know what I expected before I travelled there; perhaps a repressed population too nervous to speak out against authority and perhaps a little wary of tourists who had only begun to visit the country in any numbers in very recent times. Yet the people were so warm and welcoming and the landscapes and culture so breathtakingly beautiful. Two occurrences on that day brought this home to me.

The first happened quite by chance. We were passing on our coach through a small village when we came across a novitiation ceremony, a unique characteristic of Myanmar culture. In their Buddhist tradition, every boy over eight years old has to enter the Buddhist Order for a week or more as a novice and, once they are 20, they have to enter the order again, as an ordained monk. Novitiation is an obligation for all parents, rich or poor, and is regarded as a great praiseworthy deed. At the same time as the young boys are preparing to have their heads shaved, their sisters have their ears pierced. It is a festival of dance, music and fun, although, with the children being so young, there were a few tears as well. We were invited into the pagoda to join the celebrations. We saw line upon line of young children, the girls dressed in the most stunning decorative costumes in every colour imaginable, with sparkling necklaces around their throats and bejewelled tiaras on their young heads. It really looked like a ceremony where no expense had been spared, yet many of these people were poor beyond belief.

The other highlight of that day was an afternoon visit to Minnanthu, a typical village in the interior of Myanmar where there was no electricity or running water. The people lived in large family groups covering three or four generations. While fathers laboured out in the fields and mothers sat weaving new clothes for the family, the older children would be sent to the well, carrying back two large yellow drums of water attached to a tree branch held across their shoulders. Two tiny boys, too young for formal schooling, played idly on a home-made swing hanging from the matted ceiling of intertwined leaves. Under the very same roof, and within feet of the young boys, the family's cattle sheltered from the relentless sun. It was such a primitive existence and yet there was enormous pride, the walls of the house decorated with photographs of graduations and novitiation ceremonies.

A lady showed us how the thanaka paste was prepared, putting several drops of water on to a circular grindstone and then rubbing a thanaka wood cutting, in a circular motion, the friction producing the paste which she then applied to our faces so that we could feel its cooling properties. In the dark corner of a hut, an elderly lady puffed gently at a pipe with the most enormous bowl, its aromatic-smelling contents smouldering within.

The dusty trail outside the dwellings carried a succession of cattle-drawn carts bringing in the harvest and on the opposite side was the village school. It was a school as I remember from my own early school days, only many decades later. The children sat at individual wooden desks, each carrying the name of a donor who had helped resource the school. They had no computers or tablets, but pen, paper, blackboards and chalk. Thanaka-painted faces sat quietly working at their tasks, the classroom walls adorned with the profits of their labours. In another classroom older boys stood upright, reciting a Burmese poem of welcome to us, and I genuinely believe they meant it even if we couldn't understand the words they were speaking.

* * * * *

But now it was time for business – let the running commence. As ever, I had researched the likely conditions I would encounter during the race and hoped I had brought everything I needed with me. The distance wasn't a problem as it was 'only' a half marathon for me. The terrain was unknown but part was on road, and the off-road sections were unlikely to be as hazardous as many I had faced in the past. My main adversaries were going to be heat, humidity, insect bites and, oh yes, snakes. In the end, as in Sri Lanka, I didn't encounter any snakes, although my friend Ollie did produce a photograph of a particularly fine example slithering through a village.

In the hot and humid conditions forecast, hydration would be paramount, so I had brought my Camelbak for drinking on the run even though I knew there would be water provided en route. For me, it is much better on the stomach to take frequent sips rather than infrequent gulps. Sun protection, sunglasses, a peaked cap and insect repellent were all laid out with my vest and shorts along with the number and timing chip that we had picked up at the pasta party on the eve of the race.

* * * * *

For once, it was Jeffrey getting the lie-in as the alarm call came at 4.15am on race day. A light breakfast with Henrik and Malin, and then we climbed aboard the bus that would take us to the start at the towering and beautifully ornate Htilominlo Temple, where we arrived still in darkness. As the first light of dawn slowly broke through, the competitors gathered together and liberally applied sun tan lotion and insect repellent for the challenge ahead. A local gentleman passed among us to apply a sticky paper badge to the front of our running vests to show support for a local charity that would receive funding from the race and would be tackling the problems caused by widespread dumping of litter and waste in the region. Just as in Yangon, the villages around Bagan had fetid piles of rubbish dumped at their perimeters. Rubbish attracts rats, and rats attract snakes.

There was just time for a few pre-race photographs with the magnificent temple in the background before a brief countdown set us on our way. Just 90 competitors from 21 different countries set out on the route that would take us along sandy trails, through remote villages and past dozens of ancient temples and pagodas. For the first half hour, as the sun slowly rose in the sky, the temperature was relatively comfortable. After that, the humidity gradually took its toll as the temperature climbed towards the high 30s and, not for the first time, I felt sympathy for those facing the full marathon distance in those conditions.

There was an early setback. With the heat becoming increasingly oppressive, I was glad of my decision to wear the Camelbak so that I could drink regularly. The tube carrying the water from the reservoir to the bite-valve at its end was insulated, keeping the water cool, even in these hottest of conditions. It was just a question of flipping the cover off the bite valve, taking a few sips and replacing the thick, insulated cover again. After fewer than three miles, I started to feel water trickling down my leg. I stopped briefly to check that I had secured the cover properly but, to my consternation, discovered that I had somehow lost the bite-valve altogether in pulling and pushing the cover on and off. I was not going to go back to look for it. There was now nothing to stop the entire contents of my Camelbak siphoning out, other than the thumb of my right hand, but that's the way it was. I, at least, had the consolation of knowing that there would be further water stations en route where I could top up the reservoir if necessary. It was an inconvenience but not a disaster.

* * * * *

The sandy route turned to a narrow, rocky trail and I was joined for a while by a local runner, probably of similar age to myself.

He grinned, pointing to his chest. 'Win,' he said, and the grin grew wider.

'Doug,' I replied and we briefly shook hands as we ran.

'Win' was running bare-footed on that rocky trail. How on earth could he do it? The soles of his feet must have been made of toughened leather but, after a while, he moved ahead of me and I never caught him again.

I was joined by Steve, a tall, friendly Aussie and, as we ran together through the maze of temples, we exchanged banter of races past and present, even pausing briefly for a selfie! Then, he too ran on but I was comfortable at the pace I was running at.

From time to time, the solitude of the trail sections would be broken briefly as we passed through remote villages. The population seemed to consist entirely of elderly people and their grandchildren; presumably, the generation in between were out working in the fields. Despite the obvious poverty of their surroundings, the welcome was warm and friendly, the small children sitting cross-legged at the side of the path, tracing pictures into the sandy soil with small twigs.

The route separated between the half-marathoners and those running the full distance, and now I was much more isolated. The temperature continued to climb and my thumb continued to push down on to the end of my precious drinking tube. I entered another village and the reception was ecstatic; wild applause from the people and frenzied barking from the dogs. I waved and smiled in acknowledgement but as I began to run out beyond the village, the clamour from the crowd began to increase even further. I felt a tap on my shoulder. It was a young man gesticulating wildly. Eventually the penny dropped. In the excitement of the welcome, I had missed a small sign indicating a left turn in the village. I thanked those who had put me back on the right track, even high-fiving a couple of military policemen who were standing at the roadside.

Further on, the narrow path was interrupted by what can only be described as a small crater, maybe eight feet deep. There was no way round it; dense bush either side and with the possibility of snakes lying in wait, I wasn't going to go there. It was just a question of dropping down into the crater and then hauling myself out the other side.

As I approached the final stages of the race, more of the route was on tarmac and I was able to coax a bit more pace out of my tired legs. By now, the hot sunshine was bouncing off the surface and it was with a sense of relief that I took the final turn a mile from the Htilominlo Temple, from where we had started. Directing us on to the correct route for the finishing straight, and among the hundreds of tourists who had now arrived to view the temple was, once again, Henrik Christiansen, the former winner of the London Marathon who had manned one of the aid stations when I ran in Greenland. Turning the final bend, and seeing the finish banner 200 yards ahead, I finally released my thumb from the end of the drinking tube and raised my arms in triumph, knowing that I had comfortably beaten my time in my other exotic half marathon adventures in Petra, South Africa and Greenland. There was still just enough water left to trickle down my leg.

* * * * *

A buffet meal was laid on for those who had finished and I tucked in cautiously. Some of the meaty offerings had now been baked in hot sunshine for a couple of hours and were probably best avoided. Water and electrolyte drink were on offer and I thirstily rehydrated while waiting for others to come in, particularly those brave souls who had run the full marathon in that heat. Ollie, a Geordie lad working as a chef in Australia, was first home, finding the energy from somewhere for a breathtaking final sprint, and Alma was the first lady in the 26-mile event, but there were other remarkable stories to follow.

Audrey, from New Zealand, urged along by her compatriot Suzy, managed to finish the full marathon despite a painful foot injury that subsequently turned out to be a fracture; she spent the remaining days of her trip on crutches. Nicole, from South Africa, was the third lady to finish the full marathon despite having only completed a course of chemotherapy three months beforehand. She wept openly as she finished with her husband, and most of us had tears in our eyes, too. Zoe had been confronted by a snake during her half marathon but lived to tell the tale and my dear friend Otto, the GP from Germany, had been accompanied on the majority of his marathon journey by a stray dog whom he had chatted to on the way. He had even given the dog a name – Doug! That evening, I was happy to relate that, many years ago, I had owned a cat called Otto.

It was a pretty jubilant bunch that made our way back to the hotel that afternoon to soak up the sun by the pool which, curiously, was encircled by dozens of parched pigeons drinking thirstily from its waters. I drank a couple of large bottles of local beer under the pretext it would aid my rehydration and it's fair to say they rapidly went to my head and the evening was finished off with a poolside dinner with Otto, this time washed down with some red wine. It had been yet another unforgettable day of running.

* * * * *

Some months before we left for Myanmar, some of the competitors had been able to communicate with each other on an online chat forum set up specifically for the event. One of my fellow British runners, Dave, an erstwhile traveller, said he had booked a dawn hot-air balloon flight for the morning after the race. The seed was planted but would my fear of heights put a spoiler on the experience, both for myself and anyone else in the basket with whom I was travelling? I cast my mind back to how I had felt before I climbed that shaky staircase to the top of the 600ft Sigiriya Rock in Sri Lanka and, more importantly, the surge of achievement I felt when I accomplished it. I signed up and, to this day, am so grateful I did.

It was another 4.15am alarm call, once again leaving Jeffrey snoozing in bed. After a very light breakfast, we boarded the bus that would take us, and several other runners who had also signed up, to the launch site. In pitch darkness, it was a journey of several stops and some confusion as the wind repeatedly switched direction, thus changing our eventual destination. Finally, we arrived and were seated in a circle and offered tea and coffee while the balloons were prepared. Wary of the consequences of drinking too much coffee and then spending perhaps an hour in a balloon basket with nothing in the way of facilities, I nipped off into the bushes but the butterflies in my stomach were building. When I returned, we were about to receive a health and safety briefing and I must admit I found some degree of relief in the fact that, despite the support crew being largely young men from the local villages, our pilot, Ian, was British and from the balloon capital of the UK, Bristol. Indeed, the whole operation, Balloons over Bagan, was a British one that travelled out to Myanmar each summer. Apart from the pilot's area, there were four compartments to each basket, each holding four people. The take-off and landing procedures were explained to us, and then we sat quietly watching the locals work feverishly to prepare the balloons; testing the burners, laying out and inflating the balloon with air from a pump and then, as the sun began to rise in the sky, heating the air to bring the balloon and basket upright. It was time to climb aboard. Still moored by rope to road vehicles, around a dozen red-coloured balloons looked up to the sky around us, and then, one by one, the restraints were tossed aboard, and the roar of the burner lifted the basket into the sky. The minute we were airborne, I knew I had nothing to fear. The side of the basket was comfortably at chest height and I was no more concerned than I would have been in an aircraft, which is basically not concerned at all.

The first impression was the marked contrast between the loud roar of the burner as we gained height and the calm stillness as we drifted silently supported by nothing other than hot air. As we slowly ascended above tree level, a spectacular panorama opened up in the early-morning light. Temples here, there and everywhere, their terracotta-coloured walls blending in with the reddish-brown soil in the fields that had been cultivated for crops. All around, we saw luscious green vegetation and, on the horizon, a distant blue river overlooked by grey, rocky mountains. Camera shutters clicked continuously as new buildings and villages came into view. There was even the opportunity of a hot-air balloon selfie as a small camera, operated by Ian, and held out on a hoist several metres beyond the basket, captured our joy. These were the same temples, the same sandy trails that we had run along only 24 hours earlier, but seen from an entirely different perspective that only enhanced the beauty of this region.

Occasionally, we would come close enough to another balloon to shout greetings across to its occupants, but mostly each of the dozen balloons in the sky were skilfully piloted on their own wind-driven pathway. At times, we seemed barely above the trees and then with a roar of the burner, Ian would once again expand our horizon as we soared.

We flew over another temple, a fairly large one, maybe 60ft high, and there perched on a narrow ledge next to the pinnacle at its summit was a young boy waving feverishly up at us. Goodness knows how he had got up there but we all hoped he made it safely down. And then we were passing directly over our own hotel, the blue waters of the swimming pool shimmering in the sunshine. Guests and staff stood outside the reception entrance pointing upwards, although we were rather too high to see if we could recognise any of our non-flying compatriots.

By now, the sun had risen sufficiently to cast a huge balloon-shaped shadow across the landscape as we drifted on but, all too soon, it was time to come back down to earth, in more ways than one. The direction of the balloon was, of course, dictated by the winds and Ian was in constant radio contact with his ground crew as he searched for a suitable landing site. Eventually, he identified a field in the shadow of a large temple and directed his crew and their vehicles towards it. As we drifted slowly downwards, it was time to adopt the landing position. Seated on the floor of the basket with our backs to the direction of travel, we grasped leather handles, waiting for the moment of impact with the ground. Of course, no longer being able to see outside, we couldn't anticipate when this would be. There was a loud bump and some soil came flying into the basket. For a moment, we were airborne again and then there was a succession of further bumps, the gaps between them becoming shorter. Several sets of fingers appeared over the rim of the basket, followed, a few seconds later, by the smiley faces of the young red-uniformed men who made up the ground crew. We were down.

As the balloon was rapidly deflated and expertly packed away, we were helped from the basket and led to tables and chairs, where a breakfast of croissants and fruit, washed down with champagne, was waiting for us. Around us, local villagers gathered, laying out their displays of arts and crafts in the hope of a little extra income and I was happy to purchase a colourful sand painting of local birdlife to add to my display of memorabilia from my many running trips overseas. The hot-air balloon ride had been an unforgettable experience and one that I was so happy I had signed up for.

To run with friends among the beautiful temples and to view them from the skies was indeed a privilege, but there still seemed to be a piece of the jigsaw missing and, for me, that required a period of solitude and reflection. Why were they there? Why so many? I had no hope of coming up with any answers but later that morning I took myself out for a couple of hours and just wandered alone, in and among them. The simplicity and tranquillity of the interiors; statuettes of Buddha pointing to the four points of the compass. I just relaxed inside wondering who had sat there before me and it seemed to bring an inner peace.

* * * * *

Just one final excursion; first to a lacquerware workshop where Sun Sun once again explained the intricacies of the process as workers sat cross-legged on the floor weaving thin ribbons of bamboo into trays, plates or bowl shapes, covering them in layers of different-coloured lacquers before the final shiny black covering was applied and the product baked in the oven.

Skilled artists, with a sharp, pointed tool, would then scratch away at the layers until they reached the colour they were looking for, carving intricate, multi-coloured designs on the shiny black background. They worked with breathtaking speed and accuracy, and it was only by watching them that you began to appreciate the amount of work that had gone into the finished products that we took home as souvenirs.

The Ananda Temple. Large black and gold bells hung outside, suspended by multi-coloured ropes. The spires and pinarettes of the roof were decorated with statues of dragons and gargoyles. Inside, a monk clad in his red tunic muttered prayers to the golden Buddha statue he was kneeling before, feverishly working a string of black beads between his fingers. Just yards away, a stray black dog was being mercilessly tormented by her litter of four multi-coloured puppies, bent on mischief.

And then to our very last temple to watch the sunset over this exquisite landscape. Although the temple towered high above our heads, it was largely empty inside. We climbed its internal stone staircases, which were lit only by the light of a candle on the edge of each step. Stepping out on to the upper parapets, we watched as the sun slid below the horizon, the reddening sky accentuating the terracotta-coloured walls of the temples and pagodas around us. Probably one of the finest sunsets I have ever witnessed and the Bagan temples will live long in my memory.

* * * * *

That evening, the entire group of runners celebrated their achievements in the gardens of our hotel. A lavish Burmese buffet was laid out on long tables decorated with golden fabric. Free draught beer was on offer, too, although initially this caused problems for the inexperienced staff dispensing it, with glasses 90 per cent full of froth and only a tiny amount of liquid at the bottom of them. However, with a customer base of experienced European beer-drinkers, these problems were quickly resolved and the beer flowed freely well into the night, perhaps a little too freely for Otto and myself!

Black and gold-lacquered trophies were handed out to the leading runners and many of these were from our own party. Ollie took first male in the marathon, with Henrik, with whom I had enjoyed that fabulous evening run in Mandalay, taking second place. Alma was the winner of the ladies' marathon, with the awe-inspiring Nicola taking third place, and we also boasted the winner of the ladies' half marathon, taken by Katie, an Australian pilot.

As we drank and feasted, we were treated to an evening of traditional music, song and dance with colourful costumes, including a quite elaborate, multi-coloured dancing elephant. It had been a long day, starting with the early morning call for the balloon flight, but we had seen the very best of what Myanmar had to offer and slept soundly that night.

* * * * *

In contrast, our final few hours in Myanmar reminded us of just how much more needs to be done if the country, and Yangon in particular, seek to become a more popular tourist destination. After flying first to Mandalay, and then on to the capital, we said our farewells to most of our party and vowed to meet up again in the future. Otto and I had a few hours to kill before our respective flights and chose to take a walk around the area surrounding the airport.

It was so humid and the temperature had now soared into the mid-30s. We crossed a bridge over a small river and the waters and both banks were strewn with household rubbish. Flies buzzed around everywhere and the stench was truly unbearable. What a contrast to the beauties of Bagan. We eventually found some relief from the sun and the smell in the grounds of a Ministry of Civil Aviation building before seeking lunch at a nearby restaurant. With an already upset stomach, I opted for an apple and mayonnaise salad. Otto was rather more adventurous and went for a curry and rice, which was liberally sprinkled with hairs of unknown origin. I think we were both quite glad to get back to the relative comforts of Yangon Airport.

We bade farewell to each other, again promising to keep in touch, and then it was the long, long flight home via a very rainy Singapore. It had been another adventure that I could now tick off my list, and one that brought home to me just how much we take for granted in the lifestyles that we lead in the West.

Chapter 3

2015 and all that

From both running and personal perspectives, 2015 was an absolute roller coaster of a year. Fresh from the successful running visit to beautiful Myanmar and buoyed by improvements in my running times over a variety of distances, there was nothing but optimism about what lay ahead of me, but isn't that when life decides to bring you back down a peg or two?

All was rosy in the garden at the start of the year. *Running Hot & Cold* had been published as an ebook on Christmas Eve 2014 and the race was on to be the first person to read it and post a review. Chris, my son, won the race, although he might have had a couple of days' head start when I passed him the final edit. He had steadfastly refused to read any of the contents while the book was being written, preferring instead to read it all in one go. As days passed, the reviews began to come in and, thankfully, there was an overwhelmingly positive response. Of course, many of them were from people I knew who had been aware of the work in progress but it was particularly satisfying to see reviews from people I had never met. Even more gratifying was the fact that complete strangers contacted me after reading about how my running had helped to cope with periods of mental illness, and were happy to share their own stories and revisit their life ambitions after reading my story.

On the running front, the improved form continued. My traditional first race of the year, a local 12k on roads around Stratford-upon-Avon, with a particularly nasty hill in the middle, saw me record a three-minute personal best on an icy cold day. A few weeks later, another promising ten-mile road race produced a time that far exceeded my expectations. With everything going so well, my mind began to drift to new adventures ahead. I still had three continents left to run on if I was going to achieve my ambition of running on all seven; South America, Australia and Antarctica. The latter had seemed an impossibility on financial grounds; the cost of flying into Antarctica for a race was prohibitive, but then I discovered a race where runners could travel to the White Continent by ship, which, whilst still expensive, was just about feasible. I made tentative enquiries only to find that the race was already full for 2016 and 2017, but once a running adventure seed has been planted in my brain I find it very difficult to dismiss it. I paid a small deposit to reserve myself a place in the 2018 race, the year I would reach my 70th birthday, and what better way to celebrate that milestone than a run in the Antarctic? It also gave me the years in between to find new exploits in both South America and Australia.

My run-leading was also moving into new territory. Apart from helping others out with their Couch to 5k programmes, I now had one of my own at the local running track. A few nerves led to me messing up with times a bit on the very first week, but nobody noticed and it soon began to run like clockwork as the weeks progressed. It proved to be very rewarding. Running had given me so much in my lifetime; now I had the chance to give something back.

It was around this time that I began running more frequently with Julie, a married lady, I hasten to add. Julie was a relative newcomer to running but had her own inspiring story to tell. Like so many people these days, it was the Couch to 5k programme that triggered her interest. She started at the beginning of 2014 and ran in the sessions led by my colleague, Ernie, which I helped out at sometimes. Towards the end of March that year, she completed her first 5k in a charity run around our local lake. I was marshalling that rainy day and I remember high-fiving Julie and her daughter, Sophie, as they made their way round. But Julie did not stop at 5k. Oh no. Within six months, she had completed her first marathon in Nottingham in a very creditable five hours and 19 minutes. Such was the pleasure that running had brought into Julie's life, she now also wanted to help others follow the same path, although maybe not to full marathon in six months!

We ran together on occasions in a social running group called the Humpers, named after the fact that we ran on a Wednesday, hump day, rather than for any other reason. Julie also came to help at my own Couch to 5k sessions and, when the nine-week programme had been completed, we decided to start our own running group named 5k Maxx, as Julie was about to become a Leader in Running Fitness herself. We met on Tuesday evenings and Thursday mornings and soon built a loyal following of wannabe athletes.

It was an unlikely combination but it worked so well. Julie was less than half my age but, of the two, I was the speedier runner. I had years of running experience to work from while Julie was a relative newcomer, but we both shared the same vision of wanting to help others discover the benefits of running: physical, mental and social. I have a fairly introverted personality. Sorry for the cliché, but Julie can talk the hind legs off a donkey. In contrast to my own educational background, Julie had her 'blonde moments'. One classic that we often laugh about is when she asked, 'Is Belgium in Germany?' Most importantly, we shared a similar sense of humour and, as I would soon discover, Julie was a very caring and supportive person.

Everything was going so very well, so when I developed a bit of a chest infection towards the end of March, I assumed that, as per usual, I would shake it off within a week or two. However, something didn't quite feel right and within a week, I could sense the dark clouds of another anxiety episode beginning to creep up on me. Yes, I had felt this before, I had beaten it before and would do so again. If only it were that easy.

'What are you anxious about?' asked my GP when I paid him a visit.

I hate that question. If I knew, I could do something about it but all too often, there is no rhyme or reason for feeling that way. I explained that my son, Chris, had recently been posted to an airbase in the United Arab Emirates for six months, but he had been sent to far more dangerous places before, so I was not any more concerned than I'd been with any other of his overseas missions. That seemed to give my GP the answer he was looking for and he quickly typed it into my notes. I'm not having a go at him; he has been excellent and a great confidant over the years, but that explanation seemed to satisfy him more than me. We agreed that it was too early to talk about going back on medication and that I would soldier on for a couple more weeks before going back to him again to review the situation.

The run leading was both a godsend and a source of anxiety. With our own 5k Maxx sessions, I would worry beforehand about all the things that might possibly go wrong, and then I would feel elated afterwards when everything went like clockwork and I could sense the happiness within the group. I also took on a new challenge at this time, offering to help the people of Evesham, a town about 20 miles away, to join our Redditch running revolution by starting their own Couch to 5k programme. The sessions were to take place on a school playing field at 10.30am on a Saturday. Of course, Saturday is parkrun day but, happily, Evesham already had its own parkrun. For the nine weeks of the programme, I could do their parkrun and then make my way to the school to lead the beginners' course. Having arranged with the school caretaker to make sure the gates to the playing field would be unlocked,

I was ready to go. For the first week, as there was likely to be quite a lot of paperwork to do, I had asked Julie, her sister Louise and their mum, Jan, to come along to help, after having done Evesham parkrun first, of course. I needn't have bothered; not a single new runner turned up.

I contacted Sue, the lady who was organising the sessions for the local County Sports Partnership, and she agreed to step up the publicity, but it was to no avail; for four weeks in a row we had no customers and eventually threw in the towel. I'm happy to report that, in conjunction with the local running club, Couch to 5k is now thriving in Evesham but, at the time, it was just another source of stress for me.

The anxiety was now causing me quite dramatic insomnia and I was beginning to lose weight at a rapid rate, both signs that it was beginning to get beyond my control again and, reluctantly, I agreed to go back on the antidepressant medication as well as signing up for a short period of sleeping tablets. As had happened with previous episodes, the medication caused things to get a lot worse initially, and I began to suffer panic attacks, which themselves needed treatment. I really felt disappointed with myself for not having the mental fortitude to overcome this, but at least had the consolation of knowing that I had beaten it before and would do so again. With Julie's help, I managed to keep our running groups going but it was becoming a real struggle.

Then I received another kick in the teeth; well, not exactly a kick. For a couple of years, I had had a lower back tooth that no longer had enough enamel to support a filling. It was causing no problem, although I knew it would eventually have to come out, leaving a gap. Of course, it waited until I was at a low ebb before deciding to play up. After a couple of days of relentless toothache, I made an urgent appointment with my dentist, who found an infection in the root, and agreed that I would have to have the tooth extracted once I had had the infection cleared with a course of antibiotics. A few days later, with my jaw swelling up, I was back again for some stronger antibiotics. There was still no relief from the pain and the swelling continued to grow alarmingly. I gave it two more days but could take no more. I walked back into the dentist without an appointment, and, when he saw my swollen face, I was immediately whisked into the surgery for an emergency extraction of the offending tooth. At least that resolved the pain, but the infection in the cavity still required yet another course of antibiotics.

I was at the lowest I had felt for a long time. The combination of the anxiety, panic attacks, insomnia and now a prolonged infection was becoming too much to bear and I knew something had to change. I made two key decisions. The first was that I needed to take a break from running and, more significantly, leading the running groups. Ever supportive, Julie, who had herself now qualified as a run leader, agreed to keep our Thursday morning group going until I was feeling stronger but, for perfectly understandable family reasons, was unable to keep our Tuesday evening group going on her own, although this did happily continue under another leader. Another one of my close running buddies was Phillipa, who herself had been through a traumatic period the previous autumn when a detached retina threatened her sight, but who was now happily on the road to recovery. These two lovely ladies got me through the darkest times between them, offering to get my shopping when I felt too anxious to step outdoors, bringing me flowers to cheer me up, and occasionally popping round for a cup of tea and a chat.

The second big decision was, for the second time in my life, to seek help from a hypnotherapist. I knew that, in time, the medication would help me recover, but it always took several weeks for any improvement to take place. I needed help now and I recalled how hypnotherapy had helped me recover from the dark days following my marriage break-up many years previously. I was lucky enough to find Mark, a practitioner who lived very close to me, and arranged an appointment; in fact, we finally had three sessions together.

As in the past, the peaceful and tranquil setting in his consulting room seemed to bring a degree of logic into my muddled thinking, helping me to make better decisions. Importantly, the sessions were also recorded, allowing me to take them home and replay them at times when the stresses were beginning to rear their heads again.

Looking back now, I can see those days as the beginning of the end of what had been a very troubled period in my life, but there was one final and very worrying twist to this episode.

Around one month after the tooth incident, and during the time of the hypnotherapy sessions, I was woken one night by a quite agonising pain on my right-hand side which I felt to be coming from bone in my lower ribs and shoulder blade. It was as intense a stabbing pain as I have ever felt and I spent much of that night trying to walk it off, with numerous visits to the bathroom as my kidneys went into overdrive with the stress. To me, it didn't feel like anything related to my heart but, by 6am, I could take no more and dialled the NHS 111 line.

It was not easy answering all the questions when in such discomfort but eventually the person on the other end agreed that it didn't have the characteristics of cardiac pain and that I should present myself at my GP surgery the moment it opened and demand to be seen. This I did and I was seen immediately, although not by my usual GP. She listened attentively as I described the symptoms, which were by now beginning to subside a little.

It was the frequent visits to the bathroom that she picked up on, and she asked me whether I had ever had a PSA test, a blood test for prostate cancer. The answer was no, but I could see what she was thinking. If prostate cancer does spread, it is usually to bone. Sometimes, my medical knowledge does me no favours and the conversation set off a few alarm bells. I was sent to have some blood taken for the PSA test and also dispatched to the local hospital for an urgent chest X-ray.

The experience at the hospital did nothing to reassure me. Without a booked appointment, I had to wait a while until I could be fitted in, and heard a succession of people assured that their results would be with their doctor within three days. Then it was my turn. With my history of chest problems, I've had numerous chest X-rays over the years so it was all done and dusted within a few minutes. I was told to wait while the radiographer checked that the film had been correctly exposed, but was rather taken aback when she returned to the room.

'I'll make sure your doctor gets the report today,' she said. 'I suggest you make an appointment to see them as soon as possible.' Oh gosh, that didn't sound promising at all. As it happened, I had a routine appointment booked with my own GP the following morning to follow up on the progress with my anxiety issues, but there wasn't much sleep that night as my mind considered the likely possibilities.

The next morning, I sat in my GP's office.

'There are shadows and pockets of fluid in your right lung that shouldn't be there, so we will need to do further tests to see whether it is anything nasty or not,' he explained.

'What about the PSA test?' I asked.

'That's normal,' he replied, and one huge weight was lifted from my head. I was to be referred to a local chest consultant, but would first receive an appointment for a CT scan. Foolishly, I googled the physician's name and, yes, he was a lung cancer specialist. I wasn't out of the woods yet.

It took another week for the CT scan appointment to arrive but, during that week, I definitely began to feel a little more positive about my health. The bone pain never returned, it really was a one-off, and my anxiety was definitely beginning to recede as the combination of the medication and hypnotherapy began to take effect.

I saw my chest consultant the day after my scan and received the news I had been praying for. There was no evidence of cancer in my lung, supported by the fact that the pain had not returned and I was feeling a little better; cancer does not get better on its own. However, I would have to have a follow-up CT scan a few weeks later as, in his own words, my lungs were 'a bit of a mess', having lots of scar tissue from my previous encounters with tuberculosis and psittacosis, and he couldn't distinguish between new and old damage.

He went on to explain that the likely reason for that night of pain, and the subsequent chest X-ray, was a patch of pneumonia or pleurisy in the right lung, quite probably deriving from my earlier dental problems. Nerves passing through the lung, apparently, can refer pain to the ribs and shoulder blade. It was an explanation I was happy to accept; a patch of pneumonia was far more acceptable than cancer.

I tentatively began to do a small amount of running again on my own as I didn't yet feel confident enough to return to leading the groups, and then life threw me one of those curve balls that it does from time to time. Out of the blue, I received an email telling me that a place had become vacant for the 2016 Antarctica half marathon; did I want it? Oh, decisions, decisions.

The 2018 race that I already had an entry for would have marked the year of my 70th birthday, but who knew what would happen in the intervening two and a half years? Another very strong reason for opting for the earlier race was that two of my friends from the 'Elephant 10' would also be on the start line. Jan, from New Zealand, would run the full marathon, while Judy, from the USA, would run the half. The prospect of meeting up with them again for yet another adventure was indeed enticing. But was my current state of health up to such a demanding event? I felt I was over the worst that 2015 had thrown at me and there were another eight months ahead to continue the recovery.

On 7 July 2015, I accepted the place but, two days later, I reluctantly withdrew again. The simple reason was that I could not get any travel insurance cover and, quite rightly, the organisers were not prepared to take you without it, given the massive costs of a medical evacuation from the remotest part of the planet. As far as insurance companies were concerned, I was still under clinical investigation until I had had the second CT scan, and my place could not be held open until then. Reluctantly, I had to let Jan and Judy know I would not be joining them on their icy adventure.

* * * * *

It is a strange but knowing feeling when something seems to click inside your head and you know you are starting to emerge from the darkness and, as I have said before, this is when running really helps me to regain what I believe to be my true personality. By the end of July, I felt confident enough to re-join Julie in leading our Thursday morning group, every one of whom were wonderfully supportive. Little by little, I began to build up the mileage again and, at the beginning of September, a second CT scan gave me the all-clear from the lung problems that had put a temporary hold on my adventure plans for the future, and I was discharged from the hospital. It was beginning to come good again.

There was one final twist in the tail of what had been a pretty dramatic year. In early October, I ran a local 10k race that, frustratingly, turned out to be a good half a mile short because of a marshalling error. Amongst the spectators that day was Stuart, a good friend and running coach who I had helped out a couple of times when other commitments meant he couldn't lead his own running group, which met three times a week in Morton Stanley Park in Redditch. Stuart wasn't running the race but was there with his family to support some of his group members.

He seemed in great spirits, so it was a surprise to read on Facebook the following day that he had cancelled his Monday morning session as he had had to go into hospital. As the day unfolded, it became clear that this was no routine visit; indeed, Stuart was fighting for his life after layers of the walls in a main artery had split apart. Loss of circulation to his left leg also left him in danger of losing the limb and it was probably only Stuart's supreme fitness that helped him to pull through. It was going to be a long road to any kind of recovery and, a couple of days after the initial incident, Julie and I were approached by one of his loyal running group to ask if we would be interested in taking on the sessions during the period of Stuart's absence. They were a lovely bunch of people who would have been devastated if their group had had to wind up, so, even though it meant stepping up our run-leading commitments from one to four groups a week, Julie and I agreed to give it a go for as long as it took for Stuart to get back. The fact that I was even able to consider taking on such a challenge meant that, in my head, I was well on the way to a full recovery after such a difficult year.

* * * * *

There was a welcome footnote to what had been a pretty dramatic 2015. I am happy to report that my trainers did finally set foot on foreign soil before the year was out, even if not in a race. Chris was now back from his six-month tour of duty in the Middle East and, along with Lynne and Holly, we were able to take a much-needed break, and some late autumn sunshine, on the Greek island of Kos. My running shoes had somehow found their way into my luggage and, between us, we all managed a few runs along the beach roads and trails of Marmaris, in between a few glasses of beer and wine, of course.

Chapter 4

Running reflections and Rio

With life, health and happiness generally moving in a more positive direction, it was time to begin to look forward to the next challenge and, this time, I really did take into account my ultimate ambition of running on all of the seven continents. Antarctica was already booked, although it was still over two years away. After my rapid U-turn on the last-minute entry for 2016, I had decided that, even if a similar opportunity arose in 2017, I would keep to my place for the following year as this seemed, to me at least, to be a fitting way to celebrate the year of my 70th birthday. So that left South America or Australia.

I have been lucky enough to have enjoyed a fabulous globe-trotting life, alongside raising a family I am very proud of, and have very few regrets. Perhaps my only running regret was having to pull out of the series of runs in the deserts and mountains of South America at the very last moment in 2009, due to my previously undetected high blood pressure. Thanks to the powers of modern medication, that problem is now largely under control, although constantly being assessed. I have coped with running in extreme heat. Running in extreme cold, ditto, but running at high altitude remained an area of concern as the risk of stroke is heightened, particularly with my history of blood pressure problems. I remembered how difficult I had found running in Tibet and, as if I needed any other evidence to deter me, news came through via social media that my friend Dave, who had been a key member of our running group in Myanmar, was in intensive care in Lima after trekking in the Andes and falling victim to altitude sickness. Happily, he was able to make a full recovery but the decision was made; if I was to find a run in South America, it would have to be at lower altitude.

It didn't take long to find the perfect fit, although compared to running in the Andes, this was a much softer option: a city half marathon in Rio de Janeiro. I didn't feel any guilt about this. I had proven myself in all sorts of climatic extremes and was, after all, of pensionable age. It was a long way to travel to run a half marathon but, as I have said many times before, the running is only part of these trips to other parts of the world and here was an opportunity to visit a vibrant city that would be only a few weeks away from hosting the 2016 summer Olympics. To cap it all, the race itself would take place on my 68th birthday. Sold!

As we entered the winter months at home, life continued to look up. I was now really enjoying my return to run leading, even with all the extra sessions I was covering with Julie. There were also many offshoots coming from the success of the ebook, not least an ever-increasing number of requests to give illustrated talks on my running adventures to a wide variety of groups, clubs and societies. Also, thanks to promotion from the publishers, I was interviewed for, and the book was featured in, several magazine articles, and there was yet another invitation that caught me slightly off-guard but led to a period of running reflection that I would like to share with you now.

When I was young, Twitter was a noise a bird made. Of course, in these days of social media, it has a very different meaning. I'm still a bit reluctant to get deeply involved in these modern styles of communication but did open a Twitter account a couple of years ago, largely to promote my book, but I'm very much a novice user. It therefore came as a bit of a surprise when my son, Chris, told me that the online running forum, UKRunChat, had asked if I could host a one-hour Twitter session during which people could tweet questions to me about the book and running in general. I did not have the faintest idea how this would work in practice but fortunately both Chris and his wife, Lynne, are Twitter experts and it was their suggestion that I should travel to their home in Telford so that we could all be in the room at the same time.

As the scheduled time approached, I sat nervously at my laptop, my personal Twitter account open in front of me. With magical software installed, Chris was able to monitor several Twitter accounts at once, including his own, mine, *Running Hot & Cold*'s own account and, of course, UKRunChat. At the appointed hour, UKRunChat tweeted an introduction to me and my book, and invited people to ask questions. Within seconds, the questions started to pour in – far faster than I could type any sort of reply. I had turned off the sound notifications on my smartphone, but it vibrated across the table we were sitting around each time a new tweet came in and, for the remainder of the hour, zigzagged erratically across the table's surface, occasionally toppling off the edge but continuing to buzz incessantly on the carpet below. There was no way I could type fast enough to deal with all the questions, so, while I was answering one, Chris would be firing other questions at me and typing a response on my behalf.

It was a frantic and tiring hour, and continued to be so for some time after it was scheduled to finish, but, as a promotional event for the book, it was a huge success with a sizeable increase in book sales during the following week.

One of the questions I was asked led to a whole series of interactions, largely from runners of the older generation like myself, and it is one I have reflected on for some time since – 'In the 35 years you have been running, in what areas have you seen the greatest changes?'

Running is a simple, natural activity and, as a form of recreation, prides itself on the fact that it is very cheap to take part in, requiring very little in the way of equipment or, at least, that is the way it was. To best address the 'then and now' question, let me take you on a couple of typical runs, the first in the early 1980s, when I first took up the sport, and the second as running is today.

The 1980s was an era when distance running was beginning to grab the attention of the recreational sports men and women after the first-ever London Marathon in 1981. There really was only one important expense and that was a decent pair of running shoes. The old gym plimsolls just weren't up to the job, lacking the cushioning and support that your feet and ankles would require on a long-distance run. Any old cotton T-shirt would suffice – we all had some tucked away in the backs of cupboards and drawers – and a pair of shorts was a pair of shorts, whatever material they were made from. White cotton sports socks were £1 for six pairs at Woolworths, and that was it – you were kitted out for your run.

As I would step out of the front door, I would make a note of the time on the lounge wall clock and then I would go out and run my designated route. Returning some time later, usually as a sweaty mess, I would again note the time on the clock and, once I had got my breath back, could calculate in minutes how long I had been running for. Of course, the other thing I wanted to know was how far I had run. If the route had been entirely along roads then the easiest way to measure it would be to drive it and use the car's mileometer to measure the distance, but what if all or part of the run had been on footpaths or cross-country? Now it was time to get the Ordnance Survey map out and to measure the route as accurately as possible. I had two ways of doing this: either using pencil marks on the edge of a piece of paper each time the route deviated from a straight line, or to use a thin piece of string. Yes, you would probably get a different distance each time you measured it but if you took an average, then you would be pretty close. If your running colleagues enquired as to how your run went then, at the very least, you would round the distance up to the nearest mile, or even add a couple of miles on for extra bragging rights; after all, they wouldn't know where you had been.

Now what if it was a really hot day, or you were planning an extra-long run? How would you sustain your energy levels? Unbelievable as it may seem, in the early 1980s water came out of a tap and bottled water was not widely available, other than speciality brands such as carbonated Perrier water. Almost all bottles were made of glass, so if you did want to take a drink on a run, it would most likely be tap water in a screw-topped glass bottle; not the lightest of things to carry. A piece of fruit was the easiest nutrition to carry – an apple, orange or banana perhaps, although you wouldn't want to leave it too long to eat it, as it would soon bruise and deteriorate with all the buffeting around.

So 1980s running was indeed a relatively cheap hobby, leaving aside the cost of the all-important trainers, but it wasn't always a pleasurable experience. A sudden downpour of rain, or even the accumulation of sweat over a period of time, would significantly increase the weight of your cotton vest and shorts, leading to painful chafing in places where you really wouldn't want it!

So, let us fast-forward more than 30 years and look at what it's like to be a runner today. There have been massive advances in three main areas: kit, nutrition and technology. Of course, these haven't all happened at once but have evolved over a period of time, and the growing popularity of the pastime, particularly in an age when obesity is increasingly becoming a burden to our health services, has seen a huge growth in the running industry market.

Let's start with kit. Trainers remain the most important requirement for a running career that is hopefully free of significant injuries related to posture and your individual running style. The wide choice can be bewildering to the newcomer: neutral shoes, cushioned shoes, shoes for the under-

and over-pronators. Getting the wrong type of shoe can be an expensive mistake, both monetarily and health-wise, and it really is worth a newcomer getting a gait analysis done at a specialist running shop.

Fabrics used for running clothes have also developed significantly. No longer the sodden, heavy cotton shirts and shorts of the past. They have been replaced by modern, lightweight synthetic materials with wicking properties. What are wicking properties, you may ask? Well, simply, they move the sweat from the surface of your skin to the outer layer of the garment, where it can evaporate off into the air. Does it work? Yes, it does – a considerable advance over past years.

Of course, running in the British climate can throw all sorts of challenges at you as we progress through the four seasons and, you've guessed it, the running industry has managed to come up with many forms of clothing to cope with any climatic eventuality. Base layers, mid layers, waterproof, windproof, compression clothing – they are all out there and you can never offer adverse weather as a reason not to run if you are prepared to spend your cash.

Running nutrition has also developed into a massive market. Not only do we now have water in plastic bottles available, but there are also products to prepare you before your run, to sustain you during a run and to help your body and muscles recover afterwards. Drinks, gels and energy bars abound, not only in specialist sports shops but in the supermarkets as well, and it really is a matter of choice finding something that suits you and your digestive system. Many, however, still remain loyal to water and a banana.

But without doubt, the greatest change to emerge over my running lifetime has been the introduction of technology. Yes, I still have a clock on the lounge wall but wouldn't dream of using it to time a run. I obviously did graduate in stages from those earliest days, starting with a fairly heavy hand-held stopwatch, progressing to a less chunky wristwatch that could be used as a stopwatch, and then moving on to a watch that could even record lap times, up to a limited number, of course. Today, my running watch tracks me every single step of the way and it is far from being the cleverest on the market. When I press the 'stop' button at the end of a run, my watch starts talking to my smartphone and this in turn sends details of the run to a distant server in the United States. By the time I walk in through my front door, those who have chosen to follow me on certain web applications, such as Strava, know as much about the run as I do. If they are impressed, they can send me kudos, make a comment or ask a question. They can see a map of exactly where I have been, including a cross-section of all the hills on the route and, if they are really interested, and believe me some people are, they can see details of the distance, the time I took, how my pace fluctuated over the run, my average pace length, the number of steps I was taking every minute (we call it cadence) and even the changes in my heart rate throughout the run.

Gone are the days when you could add a couple of extra miles to your run when bragging to your mates. Now, if I posted that I had just done a five-mile run, some smart Alec would retort that, according to Strava, it was only 4.96 miles! And heaven forbid if you were forced to walk a short section of your run; those satellites overhead would note your drop in pace and let the whole world know.

There is one further area of technological advance that hasn't really touched my running career, and that is listening to music while you are on the run. For me, one of the greatest joys I get from my hobby is listening to the sounds of nature as I move along, and sometimes the silence of nature can be just as appealing. From a safety point of view, and my hearing isn't as sharp as it used to be, I need to be aware of any potential dangers around me. If I'm running on a country lane with no footpath, hearing the approach of a car, particularly from behind, gives me plenty of time to make sure I am in a safe position. However, there are a large number of people who simply can't run unless they have music to set a rhythm to run to. There are even running playlists available for different paces during a distance run.

If I had required this sort of support back in the 1980s, then I guess I would have been carrying a small transistor radio in my hand as I ran along. Walkman tape players and iPods with earphones eventually superseded these, and nowadays you will usually find runners with smartphones attached to their upper arms listening to their personal musical preferences. And yes, this also allows you to make and receive phone calls while you are running and, believe me, it happens! I remember running in a road race when a young girl I was overtaking startled me by suddenly shouting, 'Mum, I've told you not to call me when I am racing.'

So where will it end? Will there come a time when people can go for a virtual run without actually getting off the sofa? Doesn't that rather defeat the purpose? It's certainly not for me. I must admit I still like to know how far I have run and how long it has taken me. All of the other information I now have is occasionally useful if I'm assessing my fitness after a minor illness, or if I'm trying to get myself in peak condition for a particular race, but I could get by without it.

A final thought. Increasingly these days, people are extolling the virtues of running naked! This isn't as shocking as it probably sounds, but is a modern-day term for going for a run and leaving all of your technology at home. Running for the joy of running, taking in the sights and sounds of your surroundings and not feeling pressured to up your pace because your watch is beeping at you. In fact, it would be just like running in the 1980s.

* * * * *

Other repercussions from the ebook continued to arrive and to amaze me. What had originally been intended as a memoir for my family was now touching people far and wide, and it was so rewarding to get emails and letters from people, particularly those facing mental health issues, saying that I had had an impact on the way they looked at their lives. At the beginning of 2016 came the news I had been waiting for; my publishers announced that the book would be released in paperback on 1 March that year, and this started a flurry of new activity. A book signing was arranged at my local Waterstones store, I was invited to attend a Shropshire book festival to be interviewed by the local BBC journalist and I was asked to give an outdoor *Running Hot & Cold* talk at a local triathlon event. I was also invited down to London to be interviewed live on radio by Paul Hawksbee and Andy Jacobs in the TalkSport studios, taking the opportunity to take grand-daughter Holly down with me for her first-ever visit to London. What a day that was.

This was all new to me; retirement was opening up new experiences that I hadn't enjoyed in my scientific working life, and that can never be a bad thing. I already knew that my book had been nominated in the best book category for the 2016 Running Awards, so when news came through that we had made the 12-book shortlist for the awards evening at the O2 in London, I was eager to book a place despite the not inconsiderable cost. Happily, my publishers were able to help me with this and we were rewarded when it was announced that *Running Hot & Cold* had been awarded the silver trophy, only being beaten by parkrun's very own book tracing their amazing journey from Bushy Park to present-day worldwide event. To cap a truly great night, I was even able to pick up another silver trophy on behalf of my son, Chris. The ticket prices had been well out of his reach, but his Halloween-themed Dark Run 5k, with all proceeds going to a local children's hospice, won a deserved accolade in the Fun Run category. I will never forget that Tube ride back to my hotel afterwards, clutching two large trophies and having to explain to all the young late-night revellers around me what they were for. One young lady even asked if she could take a selfie with me!

* * * * *

By the springtime of 2016, Stuart was making a startling recovery from the illness that had threatened his life, although the surgery that had been performed on his blood-starved leg muscles meant he would never return to the fitness he was once renowned for. It was thrilling to see him fighting his way back to the work he loved as a coach. Little by little, he gradually returned to leading his run group sessions again, which eased the pressure on Julie and I as we were able to cut back on the three extra sessions a week. However, at the time Stuart was working his way back in, another of our running coaches sustained a serious leg injury whilst running a marathon, which resulted in Julie and I taking on another running group for six months in nearby Bromsgrove, although this was only one session a week.

Once again, a new group of runners of varying abilities to get to know but, at the end of the day, they were only there because they wanted to be and, with positive attitudes all round, our circle of running friends grew just a little wider.

* * * * *

Now, if you have followed my running journey through *Running Hot & Cold*, and indeed the previous chapter in this book, you might be forgiven for thinking that I am a fairly sickly person as there often seems to be a worrying health scare in the run-up to a major event. The enlarged heart in the days leading up to the Marathon des Sables, the blood pressure problems that put paid to my running trip to South America, the mental problems that turned the final days leading up to the Greenland trip into a period of sleepless anxiety and, of course, the mental, dental and chest problems that pretty much ruled out any adventure running during 2015. Well, 2016 proved to be no exception.

My trip to run the half marathon in Rio de Janeiro was just seven weeks away when, after a fairly gentle ten-kilometre run around my local park, I was enjoying a cup of tea at home when I suddenly started getting quite profound visual disturbances, predominantly in my left eye. No pain, just distorted and blurred vision with waves moving across my field of view. After around 30 minutes, my vision gradually returned to normal. What should I do? We men are often accused of ignoring symptoms that may just be a prelude to something more serious. Should I just ignore it and pretend it didn't happen? Why did these things always occur when I had a foreign running trip coming up?

Having been the editor of a textbook during my working career about the mechanisms and malfunctions of the brain, I knew that visual disturbances could be a sign of a so-called mini-stroke, or transient ischaemic attack, commonly referred to as a TIA. Many might have ignored it, but I couldn't. I managed to get an urgent GP appointment that same day and this provided some reassurance. There was no obvious damage to that eye, but with the limited equipment they had available in a general practice, I was advised to see my optician as soon as possible. As it happened, that turned out to be the following day; we sometimes grumble about our health services but this was an example of them working at their most efficient. More reassurance. Once again, and this time with more sophisticated equipment, the optometrist could find nothing wrong with my retinas, but – there is always a but – she wanted a second opinion and would refer me to a specialist. This time the wait was five days, during which my vision remained completely normal.

By now, the range of equipment being used to test my eyes was more than I could ever have imagined and, once again, the specialist could find nothing wrong and said he would send a full report to my GP. I left that appointment with a real sense of relief, knowing that I could now move on and prepare for my trip to Brazil, but, as I said, there is always a 'but'!

A couple of days later, I had a phone call from the GP surgery asking me to make an urgent appointment. The specialist had indeed found nothing wrong with my eyes, but had concluded that the visual episode might well have been a mini-stroke, just as I had suspected at the time. Now, I was to be referred to the TIA clinic at a hospital in Worcester and was advised not to drive in the meantime. This was becoming a real nuisance and, for the first time, I began to think that perhaps I really should have ignored that singular visual episode. It had only lasted for half an hour and I had been running regularly with no problems since. Now that I was having ongoing clinical investigations, this would also negate my travel insurance and my trip to Brazil was once again in jeopardy.

Happily, the appointment came through fairly quickly but with now fewer than three weeks to go before I was due to fly to Rio, the fear was that I would be referred for various scans for which I would need further appointments and the sand in the timer would eventually run out. As I was not able to drive, my wonderful running partner, Julie, offered to take me and to stay for as long as it took – she may have regretted saying that later.

The TIA clinic was housed within the acute stroke ward of the hospital, and once again, I felt a bit of a fraud taking up the NHS's valuable time when there were so many desperately ill people, and their traumatised families, surrounding me.

I was called in to see my consultant and he took a brief history. I told him of my plans to run in Rio and it was such a relief to find that he was sympathetic to my concerns. In my experience, doctors seem to fall into one of two camps with regard to running, and particularly so when you reach your more advanced years. They either advise you to stop running altogether, whatever the symptoms you present with, or they recognise the benefits of an exercise programme and try to keep you going, if at all possible. Happily, this chap was in the latter category.

There were, as I had suspected, a number of investigations he wished to carry out but, if I was prepared to be patient, he would try to get these fitted in during the day between the routine appointments. I went out to the car park to break the news to Julie that she might be in for a long day, but she was prepared to wait, hastily re-organising her family commitments on her phone.

One by one, the investigations were ticked off, and then, late in the afternoon, I was summoned back to see my consultant. It was good news. My heart was in good shape and the arteries in my neck that carried my blood to my brain were in excellent condition with no signs of narrowing. In his opinion, it was very unlikely that I had suffered a TIA. More likely, a tiny clot had passed across the retina on the day in question and his advice was that I should take a small daily dose of aspirin for the rest of my life to reduce the risk of that happening again.

I was discharged and it was a green light for Rio.

* * * * *

Just 19 days later, I was sitting aboard my British Airways flight to Brazil. As ever, I was feeling a little stressed at undertaking such a long journey on my own, worrying unnecessarily about what I might have forgotten or left behind. A couple of glasses of red wine and dinner soon settled my nerves and, as I like to do on a long flight, I sat back with a good book and one that I hoped would inspire me. I had met Hollie Cradduck just a month earlier at The Running Awards in London and, having heard from her about how she had set herself the goal of competing at the Ironman World Championship in memory of a much-loved niece who had died suddenly at a tragically young age, I was determined to read the full story. *Hollie's Road to Kona* didn't disappoint and the first half of the flight passed quickly as I read it from cover to cover.

With no problems at immigration other than a very long and slow queue, not what I needed after such a long flight, an uneventful but speedy taxi ride took me from the airport to my hotel on Ipanema beach. One thing struck me immediately. For a city that was just ten weeks away from the opening ceremony of the Olympic Games, there was very little, if any, evidence that it was about to happen. No flags, banners or billboards. I remembered being in Beijing eight years before they hosted the

Olympic Games and the publicity machine was already at full throttle. Rio was going to have to get its collective finger out!

I was exhausted when I finally got to my room. It is always a long, long day when travelling west on a long-haul flight. It takes me back many years to a family holiday in the States when my son, Chris, just seven at the time, did a full face-plant into a bowl of ice cream, when he could stay awake no longer.

With most of my fellow runners arriving the following day, including my room-mate, there was just one more question to answer before I fell asleep. The range of electrical sockets available in Brazil was bewildering, and the voltage was lower, too. I'd been advised to bring along a hefty step-up transformer, which had had a significant impact on my baggage allowance. I plugged it all in: laptop go, phone go, wi-fi go! It was time for sleep.

After a light breakfast, it was time for a short orientation run along the road adjacent to Ipanema and Leblon beaches. It was a public holiday so half of the dual carriageway was closed to traffic and the route swarmed with other runners making the most of the empty road. Even fairly early in the morning, the humidity was oppressive and, after just four miles, the sweat was pouring off me. For my South American run, I'd signed up for a city half marathon but this was going to be no walk in the park.

On returning to my room, I met Everett, my room-mate for the stay in Rio. Everett was an ebullient man from Los Angeles, and we immediately hit it off. He was even older than me and was also a prostate cancer survivor. Despite that, Everett was a man for the ladies and spent many an hour telling me of his prowess in this activity! What a character, and I felt slightly guilty that, whereas I had signed up for the half marathon, Everett had had no hesitation in aiming for the full marathon, even though his training had been intermittent to say the least.

Back down in the foyer, I met another familiar face and we embraced warmly. Just a couple of weeks earlier, I had posted on Facebook about my forthcoming trip to Brazil and Alma, who had won the ladies' marathon in Myanmar the previous year, replied that she was going, too. It is always great to meet up with your running friends from abroad again.

A group of us took a taxi to Sugar Loaf Mountain, taking the cable car to the top and admiring the views down on to what is an absolutely stunning city surrounded by mountains and peaks. Quite what prompted the early settlers to build a huge city in such a tricky location was questionable but, wow, what a result.

After a much-needed drink at the top, we hiked back down rather than take the cable car and were rewarded by more stunning views of the coastline as we descended down the sometimes steep wooded track.

Back in the hotel, it was time for a late-afternoon group run with all of the runners staying there, followed by a welcome reception with a wonderful selection of snacks, local beers and wine. This was proving enjoyable and it never ceased to amaze me on these trips how quickly complete strangers become good friends, principally because they share the common goal of completing a challenging event.

※ ※ ※ ※ ※

Two days to go and I began it with another early-morning run along the beach road. A few others had been invited but didn't quite make it, presumably because of the previous night's celebrations, which had continued to the roof-top bar and pizza restaurant. Despite the early hour, the heat was already oppressive.

We toured the city by coach that day, including viewing the early part of the race route. Despite the natural beauty of its surroundings, there are parts of Rio that you wouldn't want to visit on your own, and passing through some of the favelas, and viewing the horrendous conditions in which some people lived, brought home to me the stark contrast between the glitz and glamour of Copacabana and Ipanema and the slums in which so many Brazilians led their lives. It was little wonder that there had been unrest amongst the poverty-stricken about the amount of money the city was prepared to invest to host the Olympic Games, when it had such grave social problems on its doorstep.

We drove past another stark reminder that the last-minute rush to prepare the city for a massive influx of visitors might just have seen a few corners cut in the construction industry. To the west of the city, a new walkway had been built, designed to take cyclists, walkers and runners into the centre. This innovative construction, clinging to the coastline at cliff-top height, had quickly made the news when, just a few weeks after it had opened, a section of it plummeted into the sea 100ft below, after a buffeting from stormy waves at its base, tragically taking a cyclist and runner down with it.

Once again, I was struck by the apparent lack of preparedness for the imminent Olympic Games. Even the outside of the Maracana, the world-famous football stadium that would house the opening ceremony and much of the athletics, bore no evidence of what was about to unfold. As we drove along the Copacabana beach road, our guide pointed to heaps of scaffolding and fencing on the beach and proudly announced that this was to be the beach volleyball stadium. Really? However, less than three months later, sitting in front of my TV at home, I saw that same 'building site' holding several thousand spectators as the tournament unfolded. Perhaps they had been better prepared than I had given them credit for.

Our coach took us towards the Christ the Redeemer statue that overlooked the city from the Corcovado mountain top; well, as near to the statue as it was possible for a coach to go. Next, we hopped on to a train that took us further up the mountainside and then, finally, disembarked to climb the many stairs to the very top. Unsurprisingly, it was very, very crowded up there and I have never seen so many selfie sticks in one place as people jostled for optimum positions for a photo to send home. Needless to say, the sheer size of the statue, at 98ft tall, was jaw-dropping when seen up so close. How had they got it up there? In pieces, apparently, and it then took several years to assemble.

And if the statue itself was not iconic enough, then the views from the 2,300ft peak of the city below, its coastline, bays and rocky outcrops were simply superb. I'd have to say it is the most scenic city I have yet visited.

There was just one further visit on a busy day before returning to our hotel – a trip to the race Expo to pick up our numbers, T-shirts and information packs. There were the usual merchandising stands but really all I wanted was a bite to eat as we'd been on the go for several hours, and dinner was still some time away. I opted for a chicken and cheese pasty before posing for those obligatory photos where you stand with your race number in front of a large poster board, telling the world that you are indeed about to run a race a very long way from home.

Just 36 hours to go until the race started. Everything was going according to plan. What could possibly go wrong?

Chapter 5

Brazilian bugs and butterflies

As a runner, it is sometimes necessary to make difficult decisions about whether or not to take part in a race you have pre-entered. Injury or illness can strike at any time. Occasionally, the setback may be so severe that there is absolutely no prospect of running but, more often than not, it can be a delicately balanced decision. Do you run and risk aggravating matters or do you play the safe card and opt out, risking the derision of some of your hardier running companions? There are guidelines. It's probably best not to risk it if you are running a fever; your body is already fighting hard to resist the infection. A bad head cold, a chesty cough? If the symptoms are on the chest, it's best to rest; if they are above the neck, what the heck!

There may be other considerations to take into account. With some of the very large city races, it is not in the organisers' interests to have sick or injured runners on their streets, so they may offer you a guaranteed entry to the following year's race if you pull out. But what if bad luck strikes late in the day and you have already travelled thousands of miles to run the race of your dreams?

I'd had a short rest after returning from our visits to Christ the Redeemer and the Expo, and a small group of us gathered in the hotel lobby a couple of hours later. We had identified a suitable steak restaurant, and debated whether to flag down a couple of taxis or to walk there, roughly a mile and a half. In the end, the decision was to walk there and get taxis back. As we set off along the beach road, we chatted amiably amongst ourselves, some of us taking advantage of some gentle downtime to get to know each other a little more. I was vaguely aware that my stomach was a little more noisy than normal but just put that down to the pasty I'd eaten at the Expo still being digested. It took a little longer to find our restaurant than we had expected, largely because we had walked right past it without anybody noticing, such was the depth and joviality of our conversation. By the time we arrived, I was now feeling distinctly more uncomfortable and slightly nauseous. We hadn't pre-booked a table so had a wait at the bar while one was being prepared. My younger colleagues put in a bulk order for some colourful cocktails but this would have been altogether too much for me, and I settled for a glass of water which, believe me, is a very rare occurrence.

When we finally settled at our table and started to peruse the menu, I was now feeling distinctly unwell and even reading about the dishes we might soon be consuming was increasing the nausea by the second. How could this have come on so quickly? I had felt pretty good when we were in the hotel lobby. I apologised to my new friends and said I had to get back to the hotel. Alma kindly offered to come back with me but I didn't want to spoil her evening as well, so said my goodbyes and asked the restaurant to call me a taxi.

Now we had already had some experience of Rio's taxi drivers; they appear to have no lane discipline and overtake on the inside and outside at random, throwing their vehicles around sharp bends at breakneck speeds. This was not what I needed when I was feeling so sick but someone was looking out for me – I was lucky enough to get the slowest cab driver in Rio and, although it took some time, I was able to get back to the hotel without incident and headed straight for my room and the bathroom.

I will spare you the details of the following few hours, other than to say that I don't ever recall a similarly severe episode of sickness and diarrhoea. It was absolutely awful. Mentally, I had already pointed the finger of blame at that pasty eaten at the Expo, although future events would cast some doubt on that. My room-mate, Everett, had already gone out in his best bib and tucker to dance the night away in a Rio club. Time after time, I had to leap off my bed and make a desperate dash for the bathroom. In the minutes in between, I began to consider just how long this would last and how it would end. The following morning, I had pre-booked a rainforest trip on board a jeep. That was not going to happen, but what of the race the following day? Several of my friends had already told me that this was an awfully long way to travel just to run a half marathon; well, it was certainly a long way to travel not to run a half marathon.

In the early hours of the morning, Everett returned from his night-time entertainment. He was surprised to find me awake and I started to explain my predicament but he wasn't really listening. He insisted on showing me the new dance moves he had been taught by what he described as a 'seven-foot-tall lady'. I did my best to look suitably impressed and he soon settled down into a deep sleep, oblivious to the regular journeys I continued to make across the hotel room during the remainder of the night, very little of which I slept.

As dawn broke, I received a phone message from Alma asking how I was feeling. As a medic, she offered me some anti-emetic pills she had brought with her but, by now, the vomiting had largely subsided, although I couldn't say the same for the other end. The Imodium I had taken the previous evening had had no effect, so I took another double dose. Alma kindly agreed to bring some bottled water to my room as well as some of the electrolyte drink she had bought at the Expo for her marathon. Running friends are the best.

As luck would have it, pre-race day had been scheduled as a time when we were left to our own devices as to how we wanted to spend the day. I managed to persuade Everett to take my place on the rainforest trip when he eventually woke from his slumbers, as he had nothing else planned, so all was not lost.

As the morning passed, I gradually started to feel a little better. Just before noon, I felt confident enough to leave the confines of my room and move to the rooftop pool to take some photographs of the views, knowing that a toilet was still close at hand. I then moved down to the hotel lobby, where I learned that I was not the only person in our party to have been ill; perhaps it wasn't the pasty after all! Doctors had been called to a number of competitors. Food poisoning? Air conditioning? Tap water? There appeared to be no common factor.

By mid-afternoon, I felt confident enough to take a short walk along the beach outside and by early evening I was able to join my colleagues for a pasta meal, the first food I had eaten for over 24 hours. I even managed a single small glass of beer, arguing that my body needed the salt content! My insides were still so sore and I would occasionally be bent double by waves of painful stomach cramps. I felt weak from the loss of fluid, which I was desperately trying to reverse with frequent rehydration drinks but, most importantly, the visits to the toilet had stopped and I knew as the day ended that I would at least be making it to the start line.

* * * * *

An early night, a few hours of unbroken sleep and then a 4am alarm call for race day. It was also my 68th birthday and I opened the few family birthday cards that I had brought with me. Everett had also been up and down to the toilet overnight, but insisted he would go ahead with his marathon race – a brave man. We ate croissants and drank coffee in the hotel lobby before being called to a group photograph on the hotel steps. Quite a few runners were still feeling the effects of the bug, which had affected over 50 people in the hotel, and sadly, several familiar faces were not well enough even to make it to the start line. I was one of the lucky ones after all.

The half marathon was due to start at 6.30am at Praia Do Pepe in Barra Tijuca, to the west of central Rio, and it was still dark when we arrived by coach, making our way on foot slowly forward into the starting pens. The steel barriers on either side were being very strictly policed so, once in, it was almost impossible to get back out for that last-minute pee that almost inevitably marks the beginning of any big race. Maybe I was still pretty dehydrated but, for once, that urge never came. As dawn slowly broke, we could see the spray from waves breaking on to the beaches ahead whilst, overhead, a drone drifted up and down, filming us as we waited.

A short countdown and we were away on time. Even at that early hour the humidity in the air was palpable. The road climbed away from the beach level and then turned on to a dual carriageway. The early indications were that my stomach was feeling quite settled and coping with the jarring from the running. We entered a long tunnel and suddenly the heat and humidity became really oppressive, making breathing difficult. It felt almost airless in there and it was such a relief to emerge from the other end. More dual carriageway and then yet another long tunnel. This one was altogether a different experience. Air-conditioned and, halfway along, soothing classical music emerged from loudspeakers on a platform; a nice touch.

We were now approaching the imposing headland that lay to the west of Leblon and Ipanema beaches and the road ahead began to climb relentlessly. Digging deep, not pushing myself too hard, and still I was feeling okay. As we progressed eastwards along the coastal route, high above sea level, the demolished section of the new cycleway we had seen on our city tour appeared on our right. I paused for a moment at the broken section and spoke a little prayer for the cyclist and runner who were unfortunate enough to have been on that very section at the time of the collapse, and who had fallen to their deaths.

Eventually, the climbing ceased and the road began to descend gradually towards the beaches of Leblon and Ipanema, territory I was familiar with after my recce runs before the tummy bug struck. Still I was feeling okay and as I passed the frontage of our hotel at around the halfway point of the run, there was not the slightest temptation to sneak inside. The level of support from the spectators was now a little more apparent, but still nowhere near the level you might normally expect at a big city marathon. The sun was climbing higher, temperatures were creeping up and the beaches and waves of Rio were a much greater attraction to most than watching runners struggling to cope in the heat and humidity.

It was the long stretch along Copacabana beach front that finally began to take its toll on me. My spirits were occasionally lifted by roadside classical pianists or percussion bands but crowd support was minimal and, even at this relatively early hour, the sticky heat was becoming a major problem. I drank the iced water on offer at every opportunity but now the dehydrating effects of the bug were becoming all the more apparent. I looked around for any distraction that would take my mind off how I was feeling. The beautiful architecture of Rio's finest seafront hotel, the Copacabana Palace, contrasted with the ugly heap of scaffolding on the beach itself, which would eventually metamorphose into the Olympic beach volleyball stadium.

Finally, we turned inland towards the finish at Flamengo Park. Less than three miles to run, less than a parkrun but, despite the thousands of miles I had run in the past, my bowels were now telling me that this was three miles I didn't need to run. I knew from my lecturing days that the network of nerve pathways around my digestive tract, known as the enteric nervous system, are so complex they are sometimes referred to as the second brain. Now I wasn't sure which of my brains was in charge any more. Reduced to a plod, I grabbed at every offer of liquid, occasionally resorting to short periods of walking, much as I hate to admit it for a half marathon. The roadside crowds were two or three deep now and I knew the finish was near but, even with the finish banner in sight, I had to walk a few steps up the slightest of inclines. I finally shuffled across the finish line and I can't even remember if I showed any elation. A medal was hung round my neck, I grabbed two bottles of water and then we were given a goody bag, which curiously contained a packet of spaghetti and a can of beer. I looked around for the Marathon Tours flag that we'd been told to look out for at the finish and soon spotted our tour guide, Ann, on the other side of the metal fence that separated the runners from the onlookers. I literally had to cling on to the fence to talk to her.

'Are you alright?' she asked. 'You look absolutely awful,' she added reassuringly.

'I will be,' I gasped. 'Need to find a loo.'

Ann pointed me in the direction of a long line of portaloos only yards away. I headed straight there ... and will say no more!

Once I had recovered my dignity, I made my way slowly back to the Marathon Tours meeting point and eventually some of us were bussed back to the hotel, although the speedy and erratic driving certainly didn't help my predicament. Once back in my room, I endured another hour of diarrhoea and vomiting, but then felt myself slowly beginning to recover. My mood was lifted by reading the many birthday messages that had been posted on Facebook during the day before I then went down to the lobby to welcome some of the full marathon runners back.

It was surreal down there. The hotel had been invaded by a large number of very beautiful, but wafer-thin, Louis Vuitton models who, we were informed, were in the city for a photoshoot as part of the Olympic build-up. As sweat-soaked marathon runners climbed the hotel steps to get to that well-earned shower, they had to break through a line of beautiful young women, chain-smoking, presumably in order to keep their weight down. The irony of what we are prepared to do to our bodies, in order to achieve our goals, whether runners or models?

A few of us adjourned to the poolside seats on the top floor and recounted our individual experiences on what had turned out to be by far the hottest day of our Rio visit, but there was still no sign of Everett.

When I eventually went back to my room again, he had still not returned. I was snoozing lightly on the bed when he finally came in, the full marathon medal around his neck.

'Congratulations, Everett,' I exclaimed. 'I was beginning to worry about you.'

He pulled the medal off and threw it on to his bed.

'You have nothing to congratulate me for, Doug. I didn't finish. They pulled me, and a few others, out at halfway because we were going too slowly. The girl I was running with was really mad, screaming and crying, but they wouldn't let us go on. In the end, they said they would drive us to the 40km marker and let us run the final stretch so that we could get a medal, but I didn't earn it so it will just live in a drawer at home.'

I would have felt the same and felt desperately sorry for my mild-mannered but disconsolate room-mate.

There were a mixture of emotions that evening at the post-race celebration drinks. The majority were celebrating their achievement, whether full or half marathon, but some, including Everett, were still bitterly disappointed at being denied their dreams. Others were still feeling too ill even to attend, whether they had run or not, but for me the day had a happy conclusion as the hotel had made me a birthday cake, my running colleagues sang happy birthday to me and, when I eventually returned to my room, there was even a card and a small gift, a leather passport holder, from the hotel management. For me at least, it was a happy ending to what had been a traumatic couple of days, and I could now tick one more continent off my list.

When you have travelled so far across the world to compete in a destination race, it would have been foolish not to have taken the opportunity to visit any nearby natural phenomena, and particularly any designated as World Natural Heritage sites by UNESCO. I had added an optional two-night extension to my trip to visit the Iguassu Falls on the Brazil/Argentine border and this meant another 4am alarm call the morning after the half marathon. Physically, and to a lesser extent, mentally, I was still feeling rather frail after the post-race resurgence of my sickness problems, but at least there was no more running planned for a couple of days, which would give my body time to recover fully.

First I had to say goodbye to Everett as he would not be joining those moving on. We had enjoyed each other's company as room companions. Coming from such differing ethnic, social and cultural backgrounds, the one thing that linked us was a shared love of running but that had been enough to sustain a bond. We exchanged email addresses, I commiserated once more on the outcome of his race and we went our separate ways.

* * * * *

It was a two-hour flight to Iguassu. We were greeted by large poster boards warning us of the dangers of the Zika virus and the preventative measures we could take to avoid infection. This outbreak had been seen as a major threat to the Olympic Games and we had all travelled with copious amounts of insect repellent for our stay. We were also greeted by Elcio, our local English-speaking guide, and, as had been the case with Sun Sun in Myanmar, he proved to be a fountain of knowledge and ever helpful.

A coach took us into the Brazilian side of the Iguassu National Park and then onwards to the only hotel within this side of the park – the Belmond Hotel das Cataratas, a very old-fashioned two-storey building of colonial design with a lofty pink and white tower at its centre.

The change in climate was immediately noticeable. Gone were the clear blue skies and humidity of Rio. In their place were grey clouds and a temperature drop, which had us all scurrying to our suitcases in search of warmer clothing.

I was introduced to Chris, my new room companion for the next two nights. Chris, a family man from Canada, described himself as a cyclist more than a runner. This was a great understatement! In time I would learn of his amazing cycling adventures, even into war zones, and if ever a man had a story to tell in a book, then it was Chris.

My American friend, Alma, had also come along on the Iguassu trip and the three of us, along with about 20 others in the party, were soon on our way to our first sighting of the falls. As we drove in jeeps along rutted trails through thick green vegetation, local guides told us of the range of wildlife that inhabited the park, including some threatened species such as panthers and pumas, which we hoped would keep their distance during our stay.

We were dropped off at a cabin high on an embankment above the Iguassu River, fitted with life jackets and bright yellow hooded rain ponchos, and then rode down to the riverside on a steep elevator. Here, we boarded a large outboard motor-powered rubber inflatable and set off on the Macuco boat safari. We were about to get very wet!

The speed of the boat as it was piloted down the river was quite breathtaking as we literally bounced across the surface, and we all held on very tightly. In contrast, the pilot's companion perched nonchalantly on the dinghy's edge at the bow, facing towards us against the direction of travel, and filming us, seemingly without a care in the world. Soon, we had a number of smaller waterfalls in sight and the helmsman would skilfully zig-zag the boat through the tumbling ice-cold waters, and everybody on board would either gasp for breath, scream or both. These intermittent drenchings would continue for about 20 minutes as we were interviewed by our forward mariner for the DVD that we would be encouraged to buy on our return. Was it uncomfortable? Indeed it was, but it was also great fun and the mood on the boat was one of jollity. At the end of the trip, we all changed into the dry set of clothing we had been advised to take with us, and yes, along with many others, I did buy the DVD.

So this was our first experience of getting wet at Iguassu, but if we thought we had seen the full majesty of the falls, we were very much mistaken. Iguassu means 'great waters' in the Guarani language, and that is a huge understatement. Taller than Niagara Falls and twice as wide at nearly two miles, there are over 250 separate cascades.

The following morning, we climbed aboard the coach that would take us round to the Argentine side of the falls. The Tancredo Neves Bridge over the Iguassu River marked the border, the colour of the concrete barriers at the side of the road changing from the yellow and green of the Brazilian flag to the pale blue and white of Argentina at the midpoint. Looking just a short distance to the west, to where the Iguassu River met the Parana River, we were looking into Paraguay: the frontiers of three countries visible from a single viewpoint.

Having passed through customs and the obligatory souvenir shop, we boarded trains that climbed as far as they could towards the top of the falls on the Argentine side. From the final rail station, we trekked on foot on paths overlooked by inquisitive toucans from the trees above. Man-made walkways took us across sections of fast-flowing water and occasionally we would see isolated concrete pillars jutting out of the boiling froth that had previously supported footpaths, similar to those on which we were walking right then, but that had been washed away as the ever-raging waters finally took their toll.

Eventually, we reached the Devil's Throat, a 1,100-metre wide torrent, where 14 falls combined and fell 100 metres to the river below. From the viewing platforms, we were within touching distance of the water and the noise and sheer power of what we were watching is impossible to put into words. There was a curiosity, for me at least. There were numerous butterflies within the National Park and they seemed inquisitively drawn to the fine spray at the very precipice. Time after time, one would get too close and, with waterlogged wings, would plummet out of sight. Did it survive? If it didn't, why did so many follow suit? Maybe it was a butterfly version of an extreme sport.

Later in the day, we walked the lower trails, viewing the falls from down below. Wildlife was abundant. We saw monkeys in the trees, lizards scampering at our feet and friendly-looking coatis rummaging through the litter bins for tit-bits of discarded food. Signposts warned that they carried a nasty bite! From this lower viewpoint, the perpetual rainbows that constantly illuminated the clouds of spray were much more apparent, creating a fairyland of light and natural beauty.

To cap an amazing day, Chris, Alma and I took a short helicopter ride from the Brazilian side that swooped over the entire site. Each of the viewpoints we had watched from had given us a different perspective on this incredible phenomenon, but now we could see it all within one field of vision, and it took our breath away.

It was time to begin the long journey back home the following day, but first, we had one final visit to the Devil's Throat from the Brazilian side. We walked from our hotel but there had been heavy overnight rain further upstream and, as soon as we set sight on the falls, we knew something was very different. The volume of water crashing down had increased dramatically; Elcio informed us that it was now around one million gallons every single second. The falls took on a more menacing appearance and the Brazilian side offered a catwalk out into the very centre of the Devil's Throat. Once again, the yellow capes were donned but offered little protection. From the balcony at the end of the walkway, nothing was visible through the spray and the deafening roar of the waters from all around assaulted my ears. It wasn't possible to stay there for too long but, along with the feeling of isolation I had felt in the heat of the Sahara Desert and the vast expanses of the polar ice cap, those few minutes really brought home to me the variety of experiences that Mother Nature has to offer us on our planet home.

Chapter 6

The problem with wine

With South America ticked off my list of continents, my mind began to drift forward to 2017 and a running visit to Australia. Now, Australia is a long way away, and there was no chance I was going to travel that distance to run a half marathon and then come home again. This would have to be an extended visit and would take quite a bit of planning. I had pretty much decided that the race I wanted to do was the Australian Outback half marathon in the shadow of Ayers Rock in late July, but what else could I fit in? After my run in Myanmar, I was still in touch with friends living in Sydney and Melbourne, and I also had relatives living in Brisbane. Officially, Lee and Nicky were my first cousins once removed but that was a bit of a mouthful, so we just called ourselves cousins. My first cousin, Carol, had immigrated to Australia with her husband, Terry, along with their young children, the aforesaid Lee and Nicky, many years ago.

Tragically, around 20 years later, both Carol and Terry succumbed to bowel cancer at a cruelly young age, but Lee and Nicky both decided to stay in their new homeland and build new lives. I had met Lee since then when he had travelled back to the UK for holidays and work on a couple of occasions, but that had been a long time ago and I hadn't seen Nicky since she emigrated. It would be a great opportunity to catch up with them both.

There was also the tempting prospect of including a visit to New Zealand on my trip to the southern hemisphere, and having a reunion with three members of the 'Elephant 10'. You may recall that Jan was one of the ladies who I came close to visiting Antarctica with in 2016 when I accepted that offer of a last-minute place before my subsequent hasty withdrawal. For poor Jan, that race had turned out to be a major disappointment. She had entered the full marathon, but the weather deteriorated so badly during the second half of the race that the competitors had to be evacuated back to the ship before they had completed the full distance, and they were unable to return and complete the challenge. To cap it all, Jan suffered severe hypothermia during the evacuation. Undeterred, Jan was already planning a return visit to Antarctica to complete a full marathon there, but had another major challenge in front of her before then: the 2017 Marathon des Sables.

Apart from Jan's husband, Andrew, there would also be the opportunity to meet up with Linda again if I visited New Zealand. Since escaping from the elephants, and completing the Big Five Marathon, Linda had been fighting a painful rheumatic disease that had curtailed her ability to run, but New Zealanders are made of hardy stuff and slowly but surely, Linda was fighting her way back to fitness. We had kept in touch occasionally with Skype conversations.

There were so many possibilities for the trip Down Under. I would have to see who was available, and when, before putting an itinerary together for the summer of 2017.

* * * * *

Just as you should never go grocery shopping when you are feeling hungry, you should also avoid browsing for new races to enter after opening a bottle of wine.

It was a couple of months after returning from Brazil. I was sitting at home eating my evening meal and, with no racing planned for the following day, I opened that bottle of red wine. An email dropped into my inbox. It was actually informing me that somebody, not me, had won a competition, run by one of the running travel companies of which I was a client, to take part in the Cyprus International four-day challenge in November of 2016.

'Mmmm, I wonder what that involves?' was the thought that drifted through my mind as I took another sip from the glass.

For a few years now, as my birthday count had gradually ticked upwards, I had been a little easier on myself when booking challenging events. Half marathons instead of full marathons, although I still fully intend to run another full one once I cross into my eighth decade. I had also taken a step back from the multi-day events, where you run day after day, such as I had undertaken in the Sahara, China and Sri Lanka, preferring instead single races with a few warm-up and recovery runs on my own or with friends, before and afterwards. Was I being too easy on myself? Could my body still cope with a multi-day race event?

The challenge laid out on my computer screen in front of me was not of the severity of those I'd tackled before. Nevertheless, it was no walk in the park either. Four races in four days, two on trail and two on roads, with daily distances of up to a half marathon. There was also the enticing prospect of a few days of Mediterranean sunshine in a month when the days at home are getting shorter and shorter and, although there has never been any clear correlation between the swings in my mood and the changes in seasons, a few days of warm autumn sunshine never did me any harm. Before half of that bottle of wine had been consumed, I was filling in the booking form and searching for cheap flights to Cyprus. As my son, Chris, had said once before when I agreed at the last moment to run the Rome marathon with him, I really do have the breaking strain of a KitKat.

* * * * *

It wouldn't be me if there weren't some sort of minor health scare before a foreign running trip. For the final three weeks before departure, I had struggled with yet another chesty cough, along with excessive nasal and throat catarrh, which had disrupted sleep and caused prolonged headaches, but a last-minute course of antibiotics meant I was on the mend when I finally flew out of Manchester on my way to Paphos.

It was a straightforward flight, apart from having to endure the worst bacon baguette ever; I'll spare the airline's blushes! All of the competitors were met at the airport in the early evening and transferred by minibus to the beachside hotel, which seemed very pleasant indeed. When I checked into my room, my room-mate was out, which was perhaps a good thing for him, as when I opened my suitcase I was overwhelmed by the smell of insecticide; my container of mosquito spray had broken during transit. Our room was at ground level with a patio door leading out to our terrace, equipped with sun loungers, and I hung some of the smellier items of clothing outside in the hope that the odour would soon dissipate. A quick bite of dinner and then I returned to the room to meet up with Nigel, a Welshman some ten years younger than me, who was a triathlete and had used the hotel before on training camps, so knew his way around.

The following morning, after a light breakfast, I wandered around the hotel and its floral grounds which were bathed in very warm sunshine. There really is nothing more uplifting towards the end of November than feeling warm sun on your skin. Then it was time for registration. The runners were listed in alphabetical order of their first name, which was later to turn out to be a good thing for me. I picked up my bib number, 60, and various other bits and pieces, including a red plastic whistle that we had to carry on the trail stages in case anybody got lost; ominous echoes of the Marathon des Sables there.

The race series, which was now in its 12th year, was jointly organised by the Cyprus-based Arena Sports and the UK sports travel company, 2:09 Events, run by Mike Gratton, who, the more senior amongst us may remember winning the 1983 London Marathon. In the afternoon, we sat through an extensive race briefing from Mike and Yiota from Arena, covering all four legs of the series, with maps, elevation profiles and hazard warnings for each stage. This was indeed going to be a demanding few days.

A couple of hours of relaxation in the very warm sunshine, taking on board plenty of water, and it was time for stage one, the Coral Beach 6k time-trial, starting from outside the hotel itself. On paper at least, this was to be the easiest of the four runs, less than four miles on a fairly flat tarmac route. It was the time-trial format that would make it difficult to judge pace. Runners were set off at 15-second intervals in the order of their race number. What standard of runner would I be competing against? There were the usual few who had travelled far for this race series, including from Australia and the USA, but most seemed to be British. Plenty of groups in club vests from around the UK, so you might expect a pretty high standard. There were also a large number of Royal Air Force (RAF) personnel, the RAF having a strong presence on the island. Was there any chance of me winning my age category prize for the overall series? There were some pretty fit-looking elderly gentlemen around. At the end of the day, all I could do was give it my best.

We gathered on the beach road outside the hotel to the sound of the waves breaking on the shore line. Mike Gratton, stopwatch in hand, counted down from five and set runner number one on his way. With the start list being based on name rather than running ability, there was likely to be a real mix of paces being released, one at a time. At least, with number 60 on my vest, I would only have 15 minutes to wait; some would wait almost an hour, by which time others would have finished.

As we queued in number order waiting to be released, I recognised a club vest just a few places behind me; the black, white and orange of Worcester's Black Pear Joggers, a club situated just 20 miles from where I live. 'Liz' it said on the front, which I soon cottoned on to be Elizabeth, hence her proximity to me in the queue! Liz was there with her friend, Marion, and our brief conversation was quickly interrupted by Mike calling me up to the start line and beginning my own countdown. I raced 'out of the blocks', as the saying goes, acknowledging the cheering crowds lining both side of the pathway as I ran along the beach road. Within 400 metres, I was overtaken by a runner from behind and he soon sped out of sight, and that is the way the run continued as we wound our way around the hotel grounds before running out on to open country roads. Although I was pushing my pace as hard as I could, far more people were overtaking me than I was going past but, you know, I didn't mind one bit. I was running in yet another different country on a beautiful warm autumn evening. The mountains of the Akamas peninsula towered above us as we passed by numerous banana plantations, the bunches of fruit secured in blue plastic bags to protect them from insects and other animals and, apparently, creating a microclimate inside to produce the maximum yield. They were dusty roads and were certainly not free of traffic, so we needed to be ever watchful of vehicles approaching from behind.

The low sun did cause me a few problems, particularly when the twisty course took us directly towards it. Sunglasses reduced the glare a bit but I really wished I had had the foresight to pack a visor. I managed to maintain a consistent pace on a route that wasn't quite as flat as I'd expected, and then there was a final sting in the tail as the last few hundred metres turned from tarmac to a loose and rocky trail as we turned a sharp bend around three isolated palm trees. A steep embankment took us up to the finish arch and, of the many hundreds of running photographs that I have, I don't think any have shown as much pain as I had on my face as I drove myself up that slope. Stage one done!

The setting of the finish couldn't have been more picturesque. As the sun continued to sink over the sea towards the horizon, it cast an eerie light over a large shipwreck on the beach just below. The M/V *Edro III* was a cargo ship built in Norway but flying under the Sierra Leone flag, and had run aground in heavy seas in 2011. Salvage companies had now removed all pollutants from on board but the wreck remained.

Bananas, raisins and water were in plentiful supply as we cheered the other runners home and when darkness fell, which it did very suddenly at that time of year, buses took us back to the hotel for a well-earned, meat-heavy, Greek dinner and a glass of beer. Interestingly, we had been given the option of going 'all-inclusive' by the hotel but I, along with the majority, had decided that the temptation to over-indulge on the post-race refreshments was just too great, with another three early-morning races coming up. A few, however, were prepared to risk it.

On the way back to our room, Nigel and I paused at the results board. As I had suspected at the start, there were some very fast athletes in this race series. I had finished 185th out of 222 finishers and, more significantly to me, eighth out of ten in my age group. Not a hope of an age category prize and, in some respects, that took some of the pressure off me. Nigel, on the other hand, was a close second in his age category and immediately began to plot how he was going to overhaul the leader on the remaining stages.

* * * * *

An early alarm call, a light breakfast and then we boarded a coach that would take us to the start of race two, the Akamas 11k trail hill run, one described in the race brochure as a treat for lovers of mountain running. The remaining three stages were all early-morning starts so this would be the only time we had fewer than 24 hours to recover from the previous day's exertions. Okay, it had only been 6k on road but it had been at pace for all of us and we still felt it in our legs the next morning. We gathered on the cliff tops, looking down on to Toxetra Beach as busloads of competitors were dropped off, the vehicles throwing choking clouds of dust into the air. There was the usual nervous queue for the toilet portakabins, while others stretched out on rocks in the warm sunshine, taking the weight off their legs and conserving every ounce of energy for later. We had been warned, at the pre-race briefing, that this was going to be a tough day. Now, I am not someone who usually shies away from hilly races. In my own mind, I believe I am better at running uphill than downhill, where I tend to be over-cautious for fear of falling. In races, I tend to pass a lot of people during uphill sections and then they come hammering past me on the downhill on the other side. Indeed, a member of one of the running groups that I lead named me the 'Julie Andrews of Redditch', a reference to her singing of the title song in *The Sound of Music* for those readers too young to remember that far back.

There was a brief interruption to our energy-conserving mindset when, 30 minutes before the main race began, the slower runners from the previous day's time-trial were set on their way to the raucous cheers of the other competitors. Before long, it was the turn of the rest of us and a klaxon sounded to mark the beginning of our uphill journey into the island's interior.

It was so nearly the most ignominious race start of my life. Within five metres of passing over the start timing mat, my toe caught a large stone and I was heading for a full face-plant into the rocky rubble at my feet. It was only because of the usual congestion at the start that helping hands were available to break my fall and I was able to recover some degree of composure. From that point on, I made a very conscious effort to lift my feet higher than normal on each stride. The route climbed and climbed continuously and it was soon apparent that this was a race where time was irrelevant, and where passages of walking were not just welcome breaks, but unavoidable, for me at least. The first four kilometres into the Akamas National Park were relentless on a surface covered in loose rock, and it was getting warmer and warmer by the minute. The landscape was parched with scattered trees and bushes in amongst some very hefty-looking boulders. Looking back down behind us to the coastline, the sea now seemed so far below. We reached an old barn, and here bottles of water were available, which seemed a blessing. I had thought long and hard before this stage about whether or not to wear my Camelbak. In terms of distance, I would never normally consider wearing it for anything less than a half marathon and, even then, only if no drink stations were available en route. I had decided to leave it at the hotel and that had been a mistake. Not only would this race have been easier had I been able to take frequent sips of water throughout, but carrying a water bottle in your hand when your arms were so essential to maintaining balance on a very difficult surface, was a real inconvenience.

Fortunately, after the barn, the surface became a little smoother, although the uphill gradient did not relent at all. I soon passed Susan, a lady of around the same vintage as me, whom I had spoken to at the hotel before the race. Susan had run ahead from the start, but was now bloodied and battered having been patched up at the barn after a very heavy fall. She was limping but determined to carry on and smilingly reassured me that she was in a better state than a German runner who was also undergoing repairs at the barn after another tumble.

At around the halfway point, we finally reached a summit and, for the next kilometre, I ran with freedom down a hill and, probably for the first time, took in the beauty of the scenery around me. The road skirted a mountainside and the beauty and colouring of the layers in the rock formations made me wish I understood more about the geology of this area. It was bliss but the joy of running downhill was all too short-lived. Soon, the climb began again, with a particularly steep section at around nine kilometres. It was just before this that I caught up with Marion and Liz from Black Pear Joggers. They had been amongst those who had set off half an hour earlier and we paused together for a short while to take some photos of each other, with the magnificent scenery as the backdrop.

In the final stages of the race, conditions underfoot were much kinder being largely on tarmac country roads. We passed a few isolated buildings with goats munching at the sparse vegetation outside. At the very peak of a green hillside ahead sat the little village of Pano Arodes, the finish line for the day's running. We had been warned that this stage had a sting in the tail and, as with other warnings on this trip, they were fully justified. As I entered the outskirts of the village, the road once again began to climb more steeply. The village was sparsely populated, I imagine because it must be difficult to find work in such a remote location, but a few villagers stood out at the roadside, urging us onwards up the steep hill. As we came towards the centre of the village, I so wanted to finish this stage without resorting to walking again, but my legs were like jelly. I walked just a few steps to a bend in the road, my breathing rasping like an old steam locomotive. Standing by the roadside was Mike Gratton and he urged me onwards. When a former winner of the London Marathon urges you on, you can't just say 'no, not today'! From somewhere, I found the resolve to start running again and completed the final few hundred yards to the finishing arch in the village square, overlooked by a small church. A Greek Orthodox minister sat outside welcoming each of the runners as they completed their race. It had been only 11 kilometres long but with over 2,200 feet of climbing within that distance, it had undoubtedly been one of the toughest 11 kilometres I had ever run anywhere.

It was yet another stunning sunset that evening; one of the most beautiful I can ever remember. As the deep golden sun slid towards the horizon at the junction of sea and sky, painting the atmosphere with vivid oranges, reds and purples, the silhouette of a distant oil tanker slid across its surface. Man-made and natural creations combined into one stunning vista.

* * * * *

It was yet another early start the next morning as we prepared our weary bodies for the Akamas trail half marathon. Only 205 people had recorded a time for the hill race, compared to 226 for the time-trial, so the conditions were undoubtedly taking their toll.

This time, the buses took us to the town of Neo Chorio, where we started running to the ringing of the church bell of St Minas Church. Once again, the slower runners had been allowed a head start and, yet again, the initial stages of this route took us uphill, firstly through the town's narrow streets, and then out on to another rocky trail surrounded by olive fields.

Staying upright and avoiding a trip required far more concentration than it might usually have done. The sun was bearing down even more strongly but at least we had the consolation of knowing that the seemingly relentless climbing would soon come to an end. After four kilometres, a very welcome aid station marked the beginning of a long, wide and downhill trail that swung backwards and forwards down a steep hillside, with occasional precipitous drops at its edge. Now was the moment to make up some time, although the loose, rocky surface and the fear of running out of control and over the edge of the sharp bends required a degree of caution. For this stage, I had decided to wear my Camelbak and the benefits of having a regular water intake were clear as the temperature continued to rise.

As we approached the halfway point of the stage, we finally reached the coast road, although this was still some way above the turquoise blue sea at the foot of cliffs below us. From here, a sandy jeep track rose and fell around various bays and coves as we followed the coastline south, with some of the climbs deceptively tough. From time to time, small groups of quad bikes would come hurtling past us, throwing clouds of sand into the air that we had no choice other than to run through, and I could feel the grit between my teeth as I continued to sip water down my dry throat.

It was most certainly a picturesque setting but this was another tough run and the accumulated effort, particularly over this and the previous day, was taking its toll on my performance. I slowed to a walk on some of the uphill sections. Once again, I passed Liz and Marion on this coastal section and, once again, there was a lively exchange of views about how our respective runs were progressing.

Finally, I reached Lara Bay and from here the road began to fall away down towards beach level. Ahead of me, I could see the welcome sight of the finish arch on the sands, although that was still over a mile away. That seemed to be a very long mile, much of it in soft sand and although I have encountered this on many previous occasions in different parts of the world, it never gets any easier to run on. It was on weary legs that I finally crossed the finish line and then those same legs hastily transported me to a distant portaloo as the effort of those final few miles had caused some temporary discomfort to my digestive system.

Another plentiful supply of water, fruit and raisins soon restored normality and I sat back in the glorious sunshine, watching some of our runners joining the holidaymakers at the water's edge to cool off in the sea, taking comfort in the knowledge that three stages were now complete with just a ten-kilometre road race to come.

* * * * *

It was an even earlier 8am start for the final race in the series, although this did at least carry the benefit of running in cooler conditions. The race would take place around the historic city of Paphos, which was to become the European Capital of Culture the following year in 2017. Rather unfortunately, our final race in the series was to take place on the same day, and share some of the same routes, as the Paphos half marathon, promoted by a completely separate organisation. In itself, this didn't present too many problems and even had some advantages. Our much earlier start meant we would all have completed our runs before the half marathon began. It also meant we had enthusiastic support during our race from a knowledgeable crowd of running enthusiasts waiting to start their own. Where it may have caused some confusion, and probably more so for the half marathon runners than for us, was that the route around the city was marked with mile and kilometre markers for two different races of different distances at the same time: a perfect recipe for inconsistent pacing!

In the early-morning chill, but under a cloudless sky, we gathered in the shadow of the 13th-century Paphos Castle on the very edge of a busy harbour, lined with small boats and yachts. On the face of it, this was to be a pretty flat ten-kilometre road race, the like of which I had completed countless times before, but the exertions of the previous two days of hilly trail running had taken their toll. My quadriceps were burning with lactic acid and my toes and toenails, which had never really been the same since the pounding they took in the heat and humidity of Sri Lanka 11 years earlier, had been individually taped to protect the most vulnerable areas.

Nevertheless, as soon as I settled into an early steady pace, the body's natural endorphins began to wash away any pain, although I soon began to regret the five desserts that had greedily followed my dinner the previous evening. This race, and indeed the previous day's half marathon, was open to runners who hadn't signed up for the whole series and so our numbers were boosted. In fact, Mike Gratton himself ran this particular stage and demonstrated, even in his later years, that he could still run at a pace that most of us could only dream of. The course took us along the waterfront into the Kato Paphos district, with its beachside hotels and restaurants busy even at that time of the morning, before turning inland, taking us into a more rural setting. The low early-morning sun threw our elongated shadows a surprisingly long distance across the path as drones whirred overhead filming our progress. It was now pleasantly warm, as indeed was my own mood. I wasn't running at a particularly fast pace, even by my own standards, but knew that if I could maintain it for the duration of the race, I would finish in comfortably under an hour and this was after two very tough days of trail running in the mountains of the Akamas peninsula. Yes, I was about to prove that I was still capable of taking part in multi-day events, even though the distances were not up to the levels I had run in the past.

Out on the rural roads, spectator support was thin on the ground, although this gave time for inner reflection on what a delightful setting this was for a run on a November's day, compared to the often grim reality of a late autumn run at home. As soon as we turned again back towards the waterfront area, then the backing from the onlookers began to build, and particularly so from the many in their running gear making their way to the start of the half marathon. It still amazes me how a few words of encouragement from a complete stranger can give you that little extra boost of energy just as your own mental resources are beginning to flag.

Back on the waterfront, the little bars and restaurants were now a little busier; the air heavy with the aroma of coffee and cooked breakfasts. The route itself for the race was not segregated from those holidaymakers enjoying an early-morning stroll and, at times, was quite congested, requiring a certain amount of zig-zagging to pass through the crowds, not to mention a number of cats looking for a titbit, and even the occasional vehicle. Before long, the outline of Paphos Castle came back into view as we entered the harbour district. Palm trees lined the approach road and the crystal-clear waters of the harbour, the other side of a low wall, sparkled in the sunshine. Then the finish arch came into sight and now my legs were running harder than at any time in the previous four days. I truly felt quite a surge of triumph as I crossed the line, arms aloft, to the sound of rock music pounding from the speakers. I had come out to Cyprus to prove a point to that part of my mind that had been planting doubts about what I may or may not have been capable of as the inevitable ageing process continued, and I had proved those doubts wrong.

Once adorned with a medal round my neck and a personalised certificate of achievement, I then joined the queue for a plentiful breakfast of bread, croissants and fruit washed down with a free glass of beer. Yes, even at that time of the morning! I may even have accidentally joined the beer queue twice.

As ever, there were plenty of tales to tell as we shared our individual journeys with new friends at the celebration dinner. Susan, the lady who had fallen so heavily during the uphill trail race, had also fallen during the subsequent two stages but, with her knee heavily bandaged, had still managed to cross the finish line with a smile. My room-mate, Nigel, ran a superb series of races but could never quite close the gap on the Austrian runner ahead of him in his age category. Liz and Marion triumphantly finished the final stage hand in hand and Bob, another runner from a club very close to me in Redditch, could only get the time off to run the final two stages. However, he was to return for the full series a year later, and came home with no fewer than three age category trophies: a bit of a challenge when you are only travelling with hand luggage.

And last, but not least, was the amazing grey-haired Dennis who, at over 80 years of age, completed all four stages of the event, spending more time than any of us under the rays of the Mediterranean sun. I can only hope that when I reach that age, I am still able to compete in a series of races as challenging as this was.

Generally speaking, although there are local races I take part in year after year at home, I would not revisit one of my foreign running adventures as there are just so many out there that I would still like to do, health permitting. This four-day November adventure in Cyprus may just prove to be the exception to the rule, and I certainly had no regrets about that temporary moment of weakness produced by that glass of red wine.

Chapter 7

Cutting it fine in Sydney

I have made no secret of the fact that my mental health is not as strong as I would wish it to be and there is no doubt that there is still a stigma attached to this. If you are unfortunate enough to contract a physical illness, then the likelihood is that you will receive nothing but sympathy from those close to you. That isn't always the case when it is your mental wellbeing that is frail. On several occasions in my life, I have suffered really quite severe episodes of anxiety and depression and it can be a really hard battle fighting your way back out of them. For me, the warning signs of an impending crisis are weight loss and difficulty in sleeping; I am lucky in that I am usually a very sound sleeper and the amount of running I do probably helps with that.

In recent years, anxiety has been more of a feature for me than the black dog of depression, but both can be equally debilitating. Each time I fight my way out of an episode, it leaves me with the knowledge that, if I can do it once, then I can do it again, but I can't always manage it on my own. I have already spoken about the positive benefits I have gained from hypnotherapy sessions but these, for me, have always been in conjunction with medication, which may need to be taken for quite an extended period, and long after you are beginning to feel 'better'.

A while ago, after a prolonged period of stability, I asked my GP whether he thought the time was right for me to come off the medication again. His response rather took me aback. He was happy to consider a reduced dosage but said it was the surgery's policy that, after the number of repeated relapses that I had had, they would recommend remaining on the tablets for life. How did that make me feel? Disappointed in myself, yes. Sad that I wasn't able to control my own emotions enough to cope with the ups and downs of life without pharmaceutical help. On the other hand, once adjusted to the tablets, I have absolutely no side effects from them. Without doubt, the toughest two periods of the treatment are the initial few weeks, when things can often get a lot worse before you start to feel better, and the withdrawal period. Deep down, I do hope that one day I can manage again without but, in the meantime, it is just one more little pill a day to go along with those keeping my blood pressure under control.

I have long been an advocate of the beneficial effects of exercise, and running in particular, on one's mental wellbeing. Okay, if I have been in the depths of a bad bout of depression, it is hard to motivate yourself even to get out of bed, let alone run. However, once the first green shoots of recovery can be felt then, for me at least, running is a magic remedy. Maybe it's the rhythmic nature of the activity, almost hypnotic, but being out on a run when things are troubling your mind can bring about a clarity of thought that just isn't there sitting indoors and fretting about it.

One aspect of anxiety that really annoys me, and maybe other anxiety sufferers can relate to this, is my ability to worry about things that, in all probability, may never happen. I can spend hours trying to find solutions to problems that don't exist and yet a run in the great outdoors can quickly reinstate a sensible reality to my thinking.

Happily, the link between vigorous exercise and a healthier mind is increasingly being recognised, so when England Athletics, in conjunction with the mental health charity, Mind, launched a scheme in early 2016 looking for Mental Health Ambassadors to help spread this message, I had no hesitation in putting my name forward. It was one of the best things I ever did and, along with my fellow club ambassador, Emma, has helped us, and hopefully many others too. England Athletics were looking for runners who had either experienced mental health difficulties themselves, or those with close family members who were suffering from similar issues. The goal was to integrate those who suffered from mental wellbeing difficulties into a community where running and being able to talk openly went hand in hand. We are not, and never will be, mental health professionals able to offer treatment options, but rather an understanding listener and adviser and, I am proud to say, have already demonstrated the benefits of the scheme.

One particular person I can recall was a young mum I happened to get chatting to when I was helping a colleague at the first week of a Couch to 5k programme. She had joined in the hope of losing weight and with no real expectation of enjoyment. As we chatted together, it was clear that her self-confidence was at a low ebb and it helped her when I told her that I too suffered from chronic anxiety, even though I was instructing on the course. As the weeks progressed, my new friend found she was capable of achieving things she never thought possible and not only did she run 5k at the end of the programme, she went on to run a local 10k and was also shortlisted for a county-wide BBC Power of Sport award.

Of course, as in my own case, running is not a cure-all for mental wellbeing and there will always be ups and downs in life, but once you know you have achieved something personally significant in the past, there is always that knowledge that there is no reason why you can't do it again.

One small perk of our roles as Mental Health Ambassadors was that Emma and I, along with a few others from across the country, were invited, as representatives of the initiative, to an England Athletics awards evening. This gave us the opportunity to rub shoulders with some athletic greats such as Linford Christie, John Regis and Kriss Akabusi, but the highlight of the evening for me personally was to meet Joyce Smith who was, that evening, inducted into the Hall of Fame. Joyce won the women's race in the very first two London Marathons, in 1981 and 1982, both in less than two and a half hours, when already in her forties, and it was watching inspirational performances like that on TV that first triggered my interest in the sport. She wasn't to know it, but I have so many running memories in my life to be grateful to people like Joyce for, and it was a true honour to meet her in person.

* * * * *

The early part of 2017 brought two significant milestones for me, one related to running, and the other to my other sporting passion, football. The running highpoint was my 200th parkrun, which I reached at the end of January. Now 200 was not an officially recognised milestone by parkrun; I would have to do another 50 before being qualified to wear the coveted olive green T-shirt. Nevertheless, it was an achievement worth celebrating and I did so in a fashion that was very different from the personal best time I recorded on my 100th parkrun, which has remained my fastest ever and will probably stay so. This time, I and a group of close friends, young and old, ran at a leisurely pace as a herd of elephants to celebrate my narrow escape before the 2012 Big Five Marathon in South Africa. It is occasions like these that make parkrun such a fabulous community event; you don't have to run hard every week. I ran in a full elephant costume with my herd around me wearing elephantine face masks, including Chloe, the daughter of our event director, being the youngest of the pack. A fun and memorable morning.

The other sporting highlight occurred in mid-April when my home-town football team, Brighton and Hove Albion, finally made it to the dizzy heights of the Premier League. My celebrations were, however, tinged with sadness as two people very close to me, and both lifelong supporters of the club, sadly passed away from heart disease during that triumphant season. Norman, a great human being and boss, had been the person who had brought me to the Midlands and, in doing so, completely changed the course of my life. From our very first meeting when I walked into his office at the School of Pharmacy in London for an interview, and saw the Brighton and Hove Albion mirror on the wall, there was more than a professional relationship between us. When Norman moved to the University of Birmingham, I was happy to accept his invitation to join him, and we were able to attend several matches together in the years that followed.

The other gap left in my life was my dear mother-in-law, Iris. I remained very close to her even after my marriage ended, and we shared numerous footballing highs and lows together. One match that will always remain in my memory was away to Liverpool, at their famous Anfield stadium, in the FA Cup in 1983. We travelled together by coach from Brighton, looking forward to the experience but fearing the worst. At the time, Liverpool comfortably led the Division One league table while Brighton were struggling at the bottom. Liverpool had not lost a cup match at Anfield for 63 games, but amazingly we beat them 2-1. It was, to this day, the most memorable and exciting game I have ever been to. All the way home, and it's a long drive from Liverpool to Brighton, Iris was pinching my right arm and exclaiming 'I don't believe it!' but the victory was worth the bruised limb.

We continued to progress through that competition and, after another London trip with Iris, where we beat Sheffield Wednesday at Arsenal's ground, Highbury, in the semi-final, for the very first time in the club's history we were through to the FA Cup Final at Wembley.

What a day that was. We were playing the mighty Manchester United and after a feverishly exciting game, the score was 2-2 as we entered the final moments. Iris was once again beside herself with emotion as we stormed forward one last time. The ball broke to our Scottish forward Gordon Smith and on the radio commentary, which we were oblivious to at the time, Peter Jones uttered his most famous line that has gone down in football folklore:

'And Smith must score ...'

Sadly, he didn't. Five days later we were back at Wembley for a replay; there were no penalty shoot-outs in those days. This time Manchester United beat us 4-0 and the fairytale was over, but it had been an incredible journey.

Even after I moved to the Midlands, Iris remained a season ticket holder and regular supporter at all home games and enjoyed a few seasons at the club's magnificent new Amex Stadium but, in her later years, the long journey to the ground by bus became too much, although she would still be found listening fervently to the radio on every single matchday.

* * * * *

Planning was now well advanced for my Australia trip. In the end, I had settled for a four-week visit; a compromise between visiting all the places and people I would like to, and not being an excessive burden on neighbours who would be looking after my cat, Nougat, for me. In brief, I would spend a week in Sydney, followed by a week in the Outback that would include the half marathon. From there to Brisbane, where I would stay with my cousin, Lee, for a week, before a final week on the South Island of New Zealand, for a reunion with my fellow elephant escapees. With some great help from the tour organisers, the flight schedules were put together: 11 flights in total. I needed to source accommodation in Sydney, but the Outback hotel was included in the race package and in Brisbane and New Zealand, I would be staying with my cousin and running friends respectively.

Two further issues needed resolving. There was no way I was going to be away for four weeks and only run a single half marathon. Unsurprisingly, the first thought that entered my head was parkrun. This was an opportunity to open my international parkrun account and some quick online research revealed a choice of parkruns in both Sydney and Brisbane and, conveniently, I would be in both of those cities on a Saturday morning. Sadly, Invercargill, the city where I would be staying in New Zealand, did not yet have one, the nearest being in Dunedin some two to three hours' drive away. I would have to find a plan B there. There were also businesses that offered guided running tours of many cities around the world, which could be tailored and booked on an individual basis. I booked a city run and a coastline run in Sydney and they turned out to be very worthwhile investments. The website for the Brisbane guided runs seemed a lot less professional and very out of date, so I gave that one a miss; at least I could rely on cousin Lee's local knowledge for likely running routes there, as indeed with my friends in New Zealand.

The other issue was not really related to running, but rather confronting my lifelong fear of heights. My running friend Alma from Seattle, who I had run with in Myanmar and Rio, had visited Australia for a marathon the previous year, as part of her seven-continent quest. I asked her if there were any 'must-do' activities on the trip and she mentioned the climb to the top of Sydney Harbour Bridge, although she did think it was a bit pricey.

Wow, now that would be some achievement for me. Although my legs turn to jelly in the proximity of an unprotected drop, I can usually cope with heights if there is something to cling on to. I remembered the sense of achievement I had felt after the mountain stages of the Marathon des Sables, with ropes to help haul me up the steepest sections, and also the climb to the top of the 600-foot Sigiriya Rock in Sri Lanka up a rickety staircase, with the support and encouragement from my fellow runners around me. 'Don't be afraid to scare yourself' is one of the mantras I use during my running talks when trying to convince the audience to step outside of their comfort zone.

Would I scare myself with this venture? If I waited until I was in Sydney and had a chance to view just how high the bridge was, I might well have had second thoughts, so I took that scenario out of the equation by booking the climb before I left. To be frank, I was more nervous about the bridge climb than the half marathon in the Outback!

Maybe I was being a little naïve but I honestly expected the process of gaining a visitor visa to Australia, for a three-week visit, to be nothing more than a formality compared to the difficulties I had faced in gaining entry into Russia and Myanmar on previous running trips. After all, for the following week in New Zealand, I didn't even require a visa. I couldn't have been more wrong.

The initial online application form was as comprehensive as any I had filled in, not only asking for details about me and my history, but also about those I was likely to meet up with in Australia. Not having seen my cousin Lee for many years, I had to enlist his help by email to fill in all the required details about him. And then we came to the health questions – here we go again.

'Have you ever had tuberculosis?'

'Have you ever suffered from mental health problems?'

I was brought up in the belief that honesty is the best policy, so answered these questions truthfully. Yes, I had had tuberculosis but that was 63 years ago and it has never recurred. Yes, I have suffered from episodes of anxiety and depression and still take medication for it, but I feel well at the moment. I submitted the application, along with the significant fee required, and waited with fingers crossed.

Five days later, I received the response I was half expecting. The visa application could not be processed further until I had had a full medical and chest X-ray and this had to be at a private clinic authorised by the Australian immigration authorities. More expense; significantly more expense. The cost of the trip was climbing higher but there was no turning back now.

Now and again, in circumstances like these, I feel someone is looking down on me. Once again, the young lady doctor who examined me at the clinic was a runner herself. Indeed, after comparing our training schedules and times, she agreed that I was probably fitter than she was. She gave me the all-clear and sent me off for the chest X-ray that she would need to report on. I reminded her that there would be some lung scarring from my previous encounters with tuberculosis and psittacosis; I gave her details of the CT scans I had had in 2015 after a brief encounter with pneumonia, and once again crossed my fingers.

Seven days later, the visa was approved.

For once in my life, there were no late health scares for me as the departure date loomed. Unfortunately, I couldn't say the same for my cat, Nougat. For some time she had noticeably been losing weight which, in itself, was possibly a good thing as she had always been a bit on the chunky side. Indeed, the vet had advised, on her annual examination, that she go on a weight loss diet. However, her breathing was now very fast so, just a few weeks before I left for Sydney, I took her in for a check-up.

They found two problems. She had a chest infection but this could be cleared with a week's course of antibiotics. More worryingly, blood tests revealed that Nougat had an extremely overactive thyroid and this would require treatment for the rest of her life. I already felt a little guilty about leaving her for a whole month, even though she would be in her own home where, from previous experience, she would be much happier than in a cattery. But now, I would be leaving her at a time when she was ill and adjusting to new medication.

The two Helens came to my rescue. My next-door neighbour, Helen, not only agreed to keep Nougat fed and watered on a daily basis but also took on the not inconsiderable task of administering a daily tablet to a cat who didn't want it, and would do her best to dig it out of any titbits it might be hidden in. Another friend and former colleague of mine from my University of Birmingham days, also called Helen, used to be a veterinary nurse and, although she lived nearly an hour's drive away from me, agreed to visit Nougat every weekend to give her a quick check over. It was a huge relief to me to know that she would be so well looked after while I was away.

* * * * *

The big day arrived with no further mishaps and the long, long journey began with a drive down to Heathrow. Anyone who has flown in economy class all the way to Australia knows that it is not the most pleasurable of experiences, even with a few hours' break at the airport in Dubai, but a comprehensive on-board entertainment system of movies and Pink Floyd music just about kept me sane, and some 24 hours later, my feet were on the ground in a new continent.

In searching for accommodation in Sydney, my priority had been to find a hotel from which I could reach the St Peters parkrun start easily, especially as the run started at the earlier time of 8am. I wasn't looking for luxury, or anything other than basic facilities; just a room to rest my head. I finally settled on a hotel in the Surry Hills district, which was basically a bar and bistro with rooms above it but, importantly for me, directly opposite the Central rail station. The parkrun start, which I would need to reach the following morning, was just ten minutes away by train. Perfect.

We had arrived at Sydney Airport in the early-morning hours and I took the train into Central station, before hauling my luggage outside to find my hotel. Like any large railway station, there were a number of possible exits but my map-reading skills were sufficiently good to find the right one at the first attempt. I immediately spotted the hotel on the opposite side of the road, although there were some very heavy-duty engineering works and cranes to negotiate in between: I subsequently learned that the city was constructing a new light railway system in the area.

I finally reached the entrance to my hotel. It was locked. I tried a few other doors, all locked. Eventually, I spotted a lady cleaning in the downstairs bar area and caught her attention. Using hand sign language the message was clear; go away and come back at 10am! I had 90 minutes to kill, so wound my way back through the engineering works to the station, where I found an outdoor café and bought a coffee and a breakfast snack. Not the most auspicious of starts to the trip and it was surprisingly very cold. I spent an hour people-watching. Commuters hurrying on their way to work, faces glued to their mobile phone screens and comically bumping into each other; a young and dishevelled man openly begging for money but only approaching young ladies. As 10am approached, I again hauled my suitcase back towards the hotel, stopping at the station to check which platform I would need for my rail trip to parkrun the next day.

This time the door was open. I met the same lady who had turned me away before. She apologised, as she thought I had just been after an early-morning beer and she would have taken my luggage if she had known I was staying. However, the news wasn't all good; my room wouldn't be ready until 2pm but at least I could leave my luggage behind this time.

After spending the next few hours exploring those parts of Sydney between the hotel and the outskirts of the central business district, including the impressive Anzac War Memorial with its stunning Pool of Reflection, and the twisted fig trees and palms lining the avenues of Hyde Park, I returned to my room and put my running gear on.

Jet-lagged from the flights but enlivened by an afternoon stroll in the now warm sunshine, my body and, more importantly, my mind just needed a gentle run to unwind before a meal and some sleep before the early start the next morning. By luck rather than by judicious planning, I discovered there was a hilly park across the road from the hotel, with paths around the perimeter and criss-crossing the interior. Being in Sydney, the outward appearance of this park resembled one that you might find in any British city, but it was only when I set out on a steady 5k run that

I became aware I was running on the opposite side of the world. The birdsong! It was just so markedly different from the birdsong at home. One of the greatest joys of running is listening to the sounds of nature, and this was a real treat. All sorts of chirps, shrieks and trills; even the crows crowed in a much more antipodean fashion, and on the ground, black-headed ibis, their long curved beaks pecking constantly for insects in the grass, seemed to be as prolific as pigeons were at home.

* * * * *

I was up really early in readiness for my first international parkrun. Even though I was probably only 20 minutes away from my final destination in Sydney Park, I have always been a person who would rather be 30 minutes early than five minutes late. If I did arrive early, I could always introduce myself to the local team. I also had to find the start area in the park; the only information I had was that it was next to the tall chimneys, but then tall chimneys should hardly be difficult to find.

I set off from the hotel with over an hour to go before start time. I even knew which platform I needed, but, when I arrived there, the monitor was telling me that the line to St Peters was closed for engineering works. Now what? I quickly sought out a member of staff and told him I needed to get to St Peters urgently. Many might think that getting to the start line of a weekly parkrun event hardly qualified as being urgent, but I had travelled to the other side of the world for this, and wasn't going to be denied. Fortunately, the rail worker came up with a simple solution: catch a train to Sydenham on a different line and from there I could get a train to St Peters coming in from the opposite direction. There was still plenty of time. I was very soon standing on the platform at Sydenham, frustratingly having passed through a deserted St Peters station, where my new train didn't stop. The monitors gave me more bad news. The next two trains back to the city weren't stopping at St Peters either, and the one after that was scheduled to arrive with just three minutes to spare before the parkrun start time.

'Was there a quicker way to get to St Peters?' I asked another member of staff and he helpfully came up with a bus timetable on his mobile phone, but this wouldn't get me there for the 8am start either. I just had to wait on the station platform for 25 minutes and pray that my train was running on time. It was.

Several minutes later, I was finally at St Peters station. It was set in a deep cutting and surrounded by tall buildings; there was no sign of any tall chimneys! I asked a young man if he knew where the parkrun started and he stared blankly back at me, as if he had no idea what I was talking about.

Then he broke into a smile, saying 'Ah, running' and pointed up a nearby slope. I raced up it and there they were: the chimneys, the only remnants of the old brickworks. About 200 yards away, I could see the runners gathering for the start but a busy dual carriageway stood between us. I pressed the button on the pedestrian crossing; in Sydney it is an offence to cross the road until you have heard the characteristic 'swoosh, beep, beep, beep' sound that tells you it is safe to cross. I waited for what seemed like an eternity but finally the signal came. As I ran towards the gathered crowd, I heard the starter begin the countdown, '3-2-1-go'! I didn't even have time to take off the outer layers of clothing that I had intended to store safely somewhere. I just joined the back of the pack and hit the 'start' button on my watch. My first international parkrun had begun and I had made it by the skin of my teeth.

If there is such a thing as a typical parkland parkrun, then this was it. A hundred metres or so of grass at the start and finish and then the remainder on tarmac paths looping around Sydney Park. Despite my very late arrival, I soon settled into a good steady pace for me and could finally relax and take in my surroundings. As one mile approached, we headed towards a significant hill, the runners ahead of me being silhouetted against the blue sky background. As I started to climb, I noticed motivational messages had been chalked on to the tarmac path to urge everybody on upwards. This, for me, was all about the experience rather than a fast time, so when I reached the top of that hill I did something that I would never do in a parkrun at home; I stopped and pulled a camera from my waist bag and took a couple of photographs. From the brow, there was an amazing 360-degree view of the Sydney suburbs and, as I caught an image of the runners behind me fighting their way up the hill, the low morning sun threw my shadow many yards across the grassy meadow.

As with any parkrun, there was constant encouragement from those I was passing and those who passed me, and it was good to reciprocate, with a couple of people picking up my English accent. All too soon, I was making the final turn on to the grass and sprinting for the finish. A respectable time for me, and one that I could have improved on if I had had time to discard some outer layers of clothing at the start and, of course, not stopped to take photographs.

For the very first time, my barcode was scanned on international territory and then I sought out the event director for a souvenir photograph and a handshake. My parkrun number 225 would always be a special one in my memory.

* * * * *

For the remainder of that day, I went to visit those parts of Sydney that were so familiar from our TV screens. Yet again, the train line to the harbour was closed by engineering works, but a free replacement bus service soon dropped me off in the central business district. Surrounded by towering skyscrapers, I turned a corner and caught my very first glimpse of the Sydney Harbour Bridge. I would be lying if I did not admit that I felt a sinking feeling in the pit of my stomach when I saw just how high it was.

It was an afternoon of discovery: exploring the ferry terminals of Circular Quay with street musicians on every corner, the cruise ship port where a gigantic P&O liner was boarding its latest cohort of suitcase-laden passengers. Then I climbed the many steps and slopes through The Rocks district, with a brick-walled staircase seemingly painted with obscure modern art when seen close up, but when viewed from a distance, forming a facial portrait of Jack Mundey, the environmentalist who fought to save this historic district from inappropriate development in the 1970s.

And then, by chance rather than intention, I came across the offices of Bridge Climb Sydney. Feeling bold, I marched inside and confirmed my place on the climb 48 hours hence; there was no turning back now.

I walked the pedestrian route on the bridge to the midpoint, vowing to myself that I would find time to run its whole length during my stay, before then climbing the stairs inside one of the pylons. Even from this lofty viewpoint, the steel structure of the bridge still towered above. My camera was working overtime; never have I taken so many photographs in a single day. Just how many different views of the bridge and the opera house could I collect? The vast harbour below was bustling with activity with vessels of every kind: warships, sailing clippers, small personal yachts and other craft and the many ferries buzzing backwards and forwards between the northern and southern parts of the city. The giant liner I had seen being boarded earlier sounded its horn in readiness for departure, and it echoed across the bay.

Next stop was the iconic Sydney Opera House. A walk around the exterior, marvelling at the way the unique shell-like curves blended together, and then taking a tour of the interior with its magnificent concert halls and listening to our guide explaining the sad and happy stories associated with its conception, design and construction. Who knew that those stunning white curves that appeared smooth in so many iconic photographs I had seen previously were actually covered in millions, and I mean millions, of tiny white tiles? I certainly didn't.

I ate dinner that evening at an outdoor restaurant overlooking the harbour. Those white tiles of the opera house slowly turned to orange as the sun sank lower behind the harbour bridge and the upper steel girders of the bridge threw their dark shadows on to the orange roof in return. Sydney was indeed beautiful.

Chapter 8

Don't be afraid to scare yourself

The following morning, a Sunday, was the first of the two guided running tours I had booked before my departure. From the beginning, I had been impressed by the level of detail the organising company required to make sure you got the run that you wanted. The pace, the distance and any particular personal interests, such as history, geology or just general sightseeing that you would like included in the run. My designated guide, Mick, was just a few years younger than me and, like me, had discovered the joys of running fairly late in life after years of playing football. I had been in touch with Mick by email for about a month before I left the UK, and we had agreed that for this first run we would meet at my hotel and cover about ten kilometres into the eastern suburbs of the city.

From the moment we met at the hotel, Mick and I got on in a way that would far outlast the two running tours; we had so much in common in terms of background and our running ambitions in later life. Mick described the Surry Hills district as 'gritty', with some of the local bars being well occupied at breakfast time, but as we climbed through the streets lined by Victorian terraced housing, it also had a unique character.

Before too long, we had left the built-up area, crossed above the M1 motorway and entered the green areas of Moore Park. This was to be the first of several souvenir photo-opportunities on the run as we paused firstly outside the Sydney Cricket Ground, the traditional venue for New Year's Day Test matches, and then to the adjacent headquarters of the Sydney Swans Australian Football League team, where I posed taking a pass of the oval ball from the sculpture of their legendary captain, Paul Kelly.

We ran on to complete a large loop of Centennial Park, pausing once again for a photograph by one of the Russian cannons from the Crimean War that had been captured by the British after the fall of Sevastopol, and then gifted to the city of Sydney as a token of thanks for their contribution to the war effort. On to the many ponds in the park, alive with birdlife, very few of which I could identify and, once again, the contrast with birdsong at home just added to the experience.

As horses and riders cantered by, we left the park again and headed back towards the streets of Surry Hills before a final run through Prince Alfred Park, the one I had discovered on my very first afternoon in the city.

Mick promised some bush and trail running for our next joint adventure, two days hence, and we parted agreeing to meet at the ferry terminals of Circular Quay for run number two.

* * * * *

It was with a mixture of excitement and a little fear that I headed towards Sydney Harbour Bridge the following morning. Slightly surprisingly, I had slept well the night before and although I woke a little early, I spent the extra time re-reading the ten psychology tips they published for those who have a fear of heights. I set off by train to Circular Quay; yes, the engineering works had finally come to an end, and then by foot through The Rocks district, taking long, slow deep breaths to calm my butterflies. As is usually the way with me, I arrived far too early for my scheduled climb and faced a nervy wait until I was informed by the reception staff that there was a vacancy in the group climbing before me, so I was ushered straight in. Result!

There were a dozen people in our group. After watching a short video of the safety procedures we were about to follow, we were ushered into an adjacent room, asked to sign a health disclaimer, and then surprisingly, but understandably, each of us was breathalysed. Next we were presented with our blue and grey climb suits, which we changed into inside cubicles before leaving all, and I mean all, personal belongings in secure lockers. Nothing could be taken on to the bridge, including phones and cameras, just in case it was dropped on to the road, rail or pedestrian ways far below. An airport-style metal detector and body scan made sure that none of us had been tempted to slip something through.

We then met our climb leader, 60-year-old Steve, who proudly proclaimed that he had the best job in the world. Standing in a circle around him, Steve took us through the procedure for fitting our climbing harnesses and making sure they were tight enough. Everything we took with us had to be secured to the harness or suit. We were each given a radio and a set of headphones so that we could listen to Steve's commentary as we climbed in file. My spectacles, absolutely essential for me these days, were securely attached to a cord and then clipped on. It was the same for the blue souvenir Bridge Climb cap that we had been presented with. A cloth bag containing a fleece, in case we became cold high up on the bridge, was attached to the harness around my waist, and even a hankie with a loop on its corner was fastened on just in case I felt the need to blow my nose. Most importantly of all, the solid black slider that would attach to the steel safety rail for the duration of the climb hung from my waist harness. Finally, we were equipped to go ... but first we had to practise what we were about to face.

In the next room, we were faced with a large steel practice gantry with several levels, and assorted steps and ladders, and given the basic safety instructions we were required to follow. Three points of contact with the bridge at all times; moving only one arm or one foot at a time. Looking outwards, not down, and not starting to climb a ladder until the person in front had cleared the top. In turn, we each guided our slider on to the steel safety rail and traversed the gantry with Steve giving advice. Now we were really ready.

We stepped outside and I felt comfortably calm. My greatest fears were with unprotected drops, but here the many safety features gave me the inner confidence that I could do this. Steve explained that once we were attached to the safety rail, we would remain in that order until we left the bridge at the end; there would be no overtaking. We sorted ourselves into an order that everyone was comfortable with, being adjacent to their friends and relatives, and I found myself about third in the queue.

Once attached, the initial part of the walk was flat as we approached the end pylons and we could look down on the pedestrians and traffic below, but not that far below. Next we came to a tricky laddered section; three successive lengthy vertical ladders took us up to the beginnings of the steel arches. Extra members of the climb staff were located here to help anyone who got into difficulties but I coped okay, constantly reciting to myself the three points of attachment rule.

Now, we were on the upper arch of the bridge and, ahead of us, stretched hundreds of steps. One step at a time, look out not down. Far ahead we could see the maintenance cranes and, at the very top of the bridge flew the flags of Australia and New South Wales. As we climbed slowly, the views became more and more amazing and the horizon expanded further. From time to time, we paused for a rest and Steve took a few photographs of us that, of course, we could purchase at the end.

Through our headsets, he told us the history of the bridge's construction; how they built the approaches, then the two end pylons and then, from either bank, the steel arches grew outwards, supported by cables. In the summer of 1930, the two halves of the arch finally met and were welded together. Sadly, 17 men lost their lives during the construction of the bridge, and Steve relayed some of the tragic tales. The working conditions the men endured were unimaginable as they clung to the structure, first heating and then driving in millions of rivets.

The commentary had taken my mind off the climb and I suddenly found myself just yards from the twin flagpoles at the top. I had done it, although I still had to get back down. I will never forget the sense of achievement I felt as I looked across the vast expanse of the city and its harbour. The magnificent opera house was dwarfed below us.

One by one, we walked across the steel gantry at the summit to the other side of the bridge and Steve took photographs of our moment of triumph. We were invited to record a ten-second video describing our feelings.

'Don't be afraid to scare yourself. It is so, so worth it,' were the words that popped out of my mouth. I had defeated a personal nemesis. My achievement would have been a walk in the park for many; it had nothing to do with running, but at that particular moment in time, I felt invincible.

The climb back down was steady and uneventful. I was lucky enough, if that is the right word, to face what Steve described as the 'full experience' as I cautiously descended the three steel ladders. Just feet from my head, but thankfully separated by a sturdy steel mesh, the wheels of a train roared by, the backdraught making me cling tightly to the handrails.

I referred earlier to the ten psychology tips the organisation had provided to those who had a fear of heights. Tip number ten was 'Reward Yourself'; and after collecting my certificate of achievement and souvenir photos, this I did with a lovely pint of cold beer and a crocodile pizza.

* * * * *

The sun was still shining and the sky was still blue the following morning when I met my run guide, Mick, at the ferry terminals on Circular Quay. He had something very different planned for this run, but first we took the ferry across the harbour to Taronga on the north bank, home of the world-famous zoo. There was much to chat about as our boat sped across the water. Mick was particularly interested in my run-leading experiences and qualification with England Athletics and vowed to see if he could follow a similar pathway as, like me, he was passionate about helping other people discover the benefits that running can bring to both physical and mental wellbeing.

Soon our feet were back on terra firma and pounding a bumpy trail through the Sydney Harbour National Park towards Bradleys Head, where we paused for the first photographs looking back over the waters to the now distant city and bridge. The trail continued around Taylors Bay, passing through the remnants of Sydney bushland and, although I could not see it, I heard my first native kookaburra. Giant termite mounds could be seen through the greenery as we followed bush paths on a fairly flat route around Chowder Head and then the coastline around Chowder Bay.

From here the going got tougher, a lot tougher, and I struggled to keep pace with Mick as we climbed steps and ran steep slopes towards Georges Head, a viewpoint that gave magnificent views of the narrow opening from the South Pacific Ocean into what is one of the world's largest natural harbours. Mick explained that, in 1770, when Captain Cook sailed HMS *Endeavour* on the very first European voyage of discovery, he named the inlet Port Jackson, but did not think it worth exploring further at the time. It was only many years later that the true extent of Port Jackson, of which Sydney Harbour is just part, became evident.

Once the harbour had become established, it was no surprise that military experts soon decided to place guns and cannons here as part of the outer defences, and we paused to visit the Gunners' Barracks, built of sandstone, and now a world-famous restaurant. Amusingly, when Mick asked at the reception desk if we could view the inside of the restaurant, he introduced me as 'a famous author from England'. At least it gave us the go-ahead!

The run continued and now we started to descend towards sea level and to the sands and rocks of Balmoral Beach. We took a brief detour out over a small bridge to visit Rocky Point Island and then ran on the sand and skipped over rock pools at the water's edge. I certainly couldn't complain about the variety of surfaces I was being tested on, and did take one tumble when a foot slipped on a wet rock but, thankfully, it was a soft, sandy landing. In a single word, the run had been exhilarating and I hope one day I can run with Mick again.

We took the bus back to Taronga together and then said our goodbyes as Mick lived on the north shore. I am a great advocate of discovering your own runs when visiting a new city but the cash I had paid on my two running tours had been money well spent; they had provided not only great company but had been educational and informative and I had some great photographs to take away with me too.

I spent the rest of that day taking in some of the other parts of the city that I hadn't had a chance to visit yet. I enjoyed the sights and tourist attractions of Darling Harbour, certainly a focus for the ongoing redevelopment of the city. I have never seen so many giant cranes within a relatively small area in any city I have visited. I marvelled at yet another beautiful sunset from the viewing platform of the Sydney Eye before returning to one of the many restaurants in Darling Harbour for a sumptuous steak meal, a beer and an outrageously large chocolate trio dessert, all of which I managed comfortably.

With just one full day left to me in Sydney, there were a couple of people I was hoping to meet up with, one from my running past and the other from the future.

Unusually in my experience, I had been given the email address and name of the runner I would be sharing rooms with in the Outback, even before I left for Australia. Some very brief research showed that I would be in very elite company. Frank, a Danish doctor, had won the 2017 Big Five Marathon in South Africa just a few weeks previously. We exchanged a few emails to introduce ourselves and considered the possibility of meeting up in Sydney beforehand. However, as things turned out, Frank was travelling with a friend to the Blue Mountains region, so we settled for meeting at the airport instead as we were on the same flight to Ayers Rock.

My friend from the past was Linda, from New Zealand, who had been in our party chased by elephants in the 2012 Big Five Marathon. I had already arranged to spend some time with Linda, and other friends in New Zealand, during the final week of my trip Down Under. A few years younger than me, Linda had developed a painful arthritic disease not long after returning from our African adventure. For two years she had been unable to run at all, a time she found immensely frustrating. Now, with a combination of medication, physiotherapy and sheer determination, she was fighting her way back to fitness. Over those years, we had kept in touch on an occasional basis via Skype and email, and when I had told Linda that I would be travelling to Australia for the race in the Outback, she decided to enter her very first half marathon since her illness began.

Linda had been in Australia for a few days visiting her daughter and family in Tamworth and planned to take the one-hour flight to Sydney later that day, before flying on to the Outback the following morning. Now the Earth has a population of over seven and a half billion people and it never ceases to amaze me how a handful of people who have met briefly through some previous experience later find themselves in the same tiny part of the planet some years later. Since our African elephant adventure, Linda had kept in touch with Jonatan, our Danish tour guide on that trip. Jonatan had not been in the party that fled the animals but had heard the full sound effects and gunfire from the nearby lodge and had feared for the group of people he was responsible for. He was mightily relieved when we all returned safely. Since that day, Jonatan had continued to be a tour guide for the annual Big Five Marathon amongst many other events, but had moved his family to the outer suburbs of, yes, you've guessed it, Sydney.

The plan was hatched that when Linda flew into Sydney, she would travel into the city by train to Central station, where I would meet her, and then we would go together, again by train, to visit Jonatan and family for a couple of hours at his home in Normanhurst, on the outskirts of the city. With my as yet unmet new running friend, Frank, out in the Blue Mountains, and Linda on her flight into Sydney, this left the morning free for one final sightseeing run around the many sights that Sydney was so famous for.

* * * * *

While the two runs with Mick had been nothing less than superb value, their very nature had meant they had been a bit stop/start as we paused for sightseeing and photo opportunities. With a tough trail half marathon only a few days away, I needed a few miles of continuous running in my legs.

Heading out early, as the route was likely to become really congested later in the day, the run began at the ferry terminals on Circular Quay and headed for the now familiar climb up through the slopes and multiple flights of steps of The Rocks, before emerging on to the pedestrian walkway of the bridge itself. The initial approach was steep enough to remind your quads that this was going to be no easy-paced jog. So far on this trip I had walked to the midpoint of the bridge, as well as climbing to its summit, but this time it would be the whole crossing, there and back. Even in the early morning, the sun was warm on my back as I approached a bridge security guard, clad in a yellow high-vis jacket, and he nodded and wished me good morning as I passed. As I ran on, I pondered what his job might actually entail, but couldn't really come up with an answer. Once beyond the flat central span, the slope started to fall away towards the northern shore and I picked up the pace, running freely, and, not for the first time in my life, having that feeling of 'wow, am I really running here?' Once above dry land again, I carried on past the green spaces of Bradfield Park, home to a former base of the Royal Australian Air Force, before doing a U-turn at the Milsons Point railway station and retracing my steps. Now that slope I had been so joyously freewheeling down a few minutes earlier developed an entirely different character as I hauled myself back up it, trying not to lose pace.

The security guard was still there, seemingly twiddling his thumbs. Again he nodded, again I wondered. Soon, I was on the downslope again. Why do hills and slopes always seem steeper when running up? The steps off the bridge and back down through The Rocks were considerably easier in this direction, although some caution had to be exercised in order to avoid a calamitous and embarrassing tumble, but soon I was back down to the waterside and the ferry terminals of Circular Quay. The crowds were still relatively thin, so not too much swerving around was needed. You could never be sure what you were going to come across down here in the way of random entertainment. On one of my evening strolls, I encountered a group of maybe two dozen ballroom dancers twirling around at the water's edge as their music boomed out from a quayside speaker. Singers, instrumentalists of every kind, jugglers, magicians and levitationists – yes, I believe that is a word – were all there.

Now my route swung to the left on the east walkway and out towards the peninsula known as Dubbagullee, on which the Sydney Opera House was built. First past a line of restaurants, a few of which I had sampled and not been disappointed. Then a mounted inscription reminding us that this was indeed sacred Aboriginal land and to respect their communities and cultures. The opera house loomed ahead, its unique curves glowing in the morning sunlight. There were more restaurants and cafés on the Sydney Cove side at ground level and these attracted quite the most raucous and, at times, violent flocks of seagulls after any titbit that might be on offer, or indeed, anything they could grab without permission from an unsuspecting diner. It briefly took me back many years to a coastal run I did in Sussex when a seagull took a particular dislike to a red woolly hat I was wearing and bombarded me continuously until I got the message and ran for shelter.

At the tip of the peninsula was Bennelong Point, named after the Aborigine who was held captive in the late 18th century and forced to act as an intermediary between the early white colonists and the indigenous people. Now I was running along the coastline of Farm Cove and into the beautiful Royal Botanical Gardens that I had spent some time exploring during my short stay in Sydney. No time to stop and admire on this occasion; I followed the path that hugged the coastline and headed out towards Mrs Macquarie's Point, the final turn of the run. Mrs Elizabeth Macquarie was the wife of the governor of New South Wales in the early 19th century, and had a bench carved out of the ochre-coloured sandstone that dominated the peninsula so that she could sit and admire the views on her daily walk. Of course, back then, there would have been no harbour bridge or opera house to admire but this viewing point does give possibly the best combined view of these two distinctive landmarks that epitomise the city and it was no surprise to learn that this was probably the most sought-after viewing point for Sydney's iconic firework display, which heralds the beginning of each new year.

Making a sharp turn down by the rock pools that lead down to the water, the final much speedier mile of the run took me back through the Botanical Gardens, back around the outside of the opera house and then, swerving through the increasingly congested pedestrian ways, to my finish point back at Circular Quay. A beautifully scenic and historical ten kilometres, run at a pace that left me slightly breathless but that only seemed to enhance the experience. It was, to me, a perfect digest of all I had experienced of the city over the past week, crammed into an hour of early-morning sunshine. Sydney had left me in an upbeat frame of mind before the challenging adventure ahead.

* * * * *

I met up with Linda at Central station later that afternoon. It was great to be back with her again after five years and we spent the train journey out to Normanhurst exchanging tales of our respective children and grandchildren. Despite the health problems Linda had been through, she was a determined lady and I could sense her eagerness to fight her way back to running fitness.

Jonatan also looked much the same as he had done five years earlier in South Africa: a tall and powerfully built man, wearing a T-shirt marking his most recent trip to the Big Five Marathon, during which the elephants had been very well behaved apparently. We were introduced to his mother and father-in-law, as well as his two delightful young children, and spent a couple of hours over tea and Danish pastries reminiscing about our past adventures together in the African bush.

After a tour of his house and garden, in a leafy suburb full of wildlife chatter, we said our farewells once more before Linda and I headed back to Sydney Harbour for a final waterside meal and a glass of wine. Our glasses clinked together as we wished each other success in the race ahead. It was now time to leave the big city lights; our next meeting would be in the Australian Outback.

Chapter 9

Red sand and sunsets

I was in an aisle seat for the three-hour flight out to Ayers Rock so couldn't get a clear view of the ground below as we made our final approach to the nearby Connellan Airport. For a brief moment, the left wing dipped as we made a turn and I got my very first clear sighting of the unmistakeable monolith below. We continued to descend over the red, parched soil, bracing ourselves for that moment of impact when the landing gear makes contact with the ground, when there was a sudden surge of acceleration from the engines and we roared skywards again. The pilot was soon on the public address to reassure us that all was well but that he had had to abort the landing because the aircraft was heavy and had met unexpectedly strong side winds. We would be going round again. At the second attempt, we were safely on the ground in the Australian Outback.

As arranged in our earlier email exchanges, I first met up with my room-mate, Frank, in the departure lounge at Sydney Airport. We got on famously from the very beginning. As I mentioned previously, Frank was a doctor in Denmark, maybe 25 years my junior, although a little disillusioned with the way doctors were treated in his home country. The medical link in our professional lives helped to smooth the early introductions. Modest, and very unassuming, Frank seemed almost embarrassed to talk about his victory in the Big Five Marathon just a few weeks earlier and was surprised when I told him of our elephant escapade, as he didn't recall seeing any. Perhaps he was moving too fast.

We had both booked our trips through the American company, Marathon Tours, who I had previously travelled with, and been impressed by, on my visit to Rio, and found ourselves seated together on the plane so that we could continue our 'getting to know you' conversations on the flight inland. Although Marathon Tours had made all the travel arrangements for us, they were not sending a representative to the race itself, which was organised by an Australian adventure travel agency, Travelling Fit, who, once again, turned out to be superb organisers.

* * * * *

As the airport at Ayers Rock was small, we were soon reunited with our luggage and directed on to coaches that would take us on the short journey to our destination hotel in the nearby resort town of Yulara. Let me pause for a minute here to give a little bit of context to some of the place names I will be using in the coming pages, as this part of the Northern Territory is very much a vast empty space. Indeed, as one of our tour guides informed us, we were actually closer to the International Space Station overhead than we were to the nearest large town of Alice Springs.

In what was an otherwise very flat landscape, there were two major rock formations, separated by a distance of around 16 miles. Ayers Rock or Uluru, as it is known to the indigenous Aboriginal people to whom it is a sacred site, is a single giant sandstone monolith standing over 1,000 feet high above the surrounding land. The other, Kata Tjuta, is also largely composed of sandstone and is a group of 36 domed rocks, the highest of which is Mount Olga, rising 1,800 feet above the plain; indeed, the translation of the name, Kata Tjuta, means

My much-missed hen family of (left to right) Tikka, Bhuna and Korma.

A special moment in any father's life. The wedding of my lovely daughter, Angela, to Ben (Halo Images).

Meeting one of my personal inspirations: Joyce Smith, female winner of the London Marathon in 1981 and 1982.

Mandalay Palace in Myanmar. The sunset run around its perimeter with Henrik, Malin and Otto is one I will never forget.

They said transport in central Myanmar was fairly primitive and they weren't wrong.

Classroom time in the village school of Minnanthu.

A finish line medal photo in front of the impressive Htilominlo temple.

Stunning views of the myriad of Bagan temples, large and small, viewed from the basket of a hot-air balloon.

Father and son trophy celebration: Chris (fun run category) and I (book category) both won silver awards at the 2016 Running Awards in London.

A running friends' group selfie at the top of Sugarloaf Mountain in Rio.

Close-up view of Christ the Redeemer.

Pre-dawn – waiting for the Rio half marathon start.

A finish line medal photo which disguises just how ill I was feeling at that moment!

With Alma and Chris at the spectacular Devil's Throat, Iguassu Falls on the Brazil–Argentina border.

Post-race refreshments after the time trial in Cyprus, with the wreck of **Edro III** *in the background.*

The relentless uphill trail stage to Pano Arodes.

Celebrating completion of the four-day challenge in Paphos with a cold beer (or two).

An oil tanker crosses the Mediterranean sunset.

An elephant-themed celebration of my 200th parkrun (Mark Berbezier).

A non-lycra photo with two of the most supportive running friends you could ever wish for (left to right, Julie, me, Phillipa).

Meeting the run director at my first international parkrun; St Peters in Sydney Park

A low, early morning sun throwing my long shadow on to the red, sandy soil of the Australian Outback.

Having baked in the sun running at its base, a more leisurely view of Ayers Rock from a helicopter above.

A post-race celebration meaty, bush barbecue with Linda.

Meeting Gareth at Brisbane's South Bank parkrun, running both banks of the river with two bridge crossings.

Just five years earlier, we had all escaped the angry elephants in South Africa. A reunion in Alexandra, New Zealand! (Left to right) Andrew, Jan, myself and Linda.

En route from a cold British winter to an even colder Antarctica and having to run at 30 °C in Buenos Aires on the way!

Waiting to board our ship in Ushuaia, the southernmost city in the world.

Scrubbing my trail shoes to ensure that absolutely nothing was introduced to Antarctica that didn't belong there.

Snowy trails, frozen lakes – the race in Antarctica unfolds.

Two hugely treasured medals; one for completing the race, the other for ticking off my seventh continent.

A beautiful whale fluke between our zodiac and the Ioffe in Mikkelsen Bay.

Yes, the humpback whales really did get this close in Cierva Cove. No zoom lens required!

To me, this berg looks like a bearded wizard sitting on the end of his own personal island! And you?

Blue ice and mushroom-shaped bergs forming a natural frame.

We were repeatedly told that the only thing we could leave behind in Antarctica were our footprints in the snow. I left a number '7' as well, to celebrate my achievement!

It really is a privilege to run with my two beautiful granddaughters, Holly and Josie.

At my 70th birthday party, with Holly and Josie.

'many heads'. To put the geology of this area into the most simplistic of terms, I can do no better than, once again, to refer to our knowledgeable tour guide, who described these two formations as 'the two ends of a giant underground banana, that have pushed up through the surface'.

In the early 1970s, tourists began to travel in numbers to this very remote region and a number of motels grew up around the base of Ayers Rock. This caused some damage to its fragile environment, so a decision was made to remove them and replace them with the resort town of Yulara, opened in 1976, which is situated outside the Uluru-Kata Tjuta National Park and has a permanent population of fewer than 1,000 people. The settlement now houses a whole range of accommodation for travellers, from basic to fairly luxurious hotels, backpacker hostels and also a camping ground. At the heart of the resort is a small shopping centre with a supermarket, some souvenir shops and a range of eating establishments, including the delightfully named Chinese noodle house, Ayers Wok.

* * * * *

Yulara is essentially a giant circular road, with the buildings around the outer edges, and a series of trails criss-crossing the central bushland. Within an hour of checking into our hotel, we were changing into running gear for a hosted warm-up run. With competitors spread out in accommodation across the resort, the run was to start at a hotel on the other side of the circle, which gave Frank, Linda and I the opportunity to feel the soft, red soil of the Outback under our feet for the first time as we trekked across. The immediate surprise to me was the amount of blue grass around, and I'm not talking music.

It was a gentle two-mile run in warm late-afternoon sunshine, culminating in a steepish climb to the top of one of the lookout points of Yulara, and our first chance to get a good look at Ayers Rock, albeit over six miles away and, if you turned the other way, to see the multiple domes of Kata Tjuta. Slightly disconcerting was the sight of several plumes of dark smoke on the horizon. I was aware before I left home of the tragic story of Turia Pitt, who had become engulfed in a fast-moving bush fire while running an ultramarathon in the Outback, and been horribly disfigured as a result. We were assured that these were almost certainly controlled fires, used to clear areas to prevent the rapid movement of wildfires but, nevertheless, it was a stark reminder of just how hostile an environment we would be running in.

That evening, all of the competitors sat at tables at the poolside of our hotel for an outdoor welcome dinner; an opportunity to make new friends from around the world and share tales of running ventures past. With a very early wake-up call scheduled for the following morning, as the plan was to watch the sun rise over Ayers Rock and then walk around its base, it was not a late night, but unfortunately for me, a disrupted one.

For as far back as I can remember, I have been blighted with an over-sensitive digestive system. When I prepare my packing list for running trips abroad, the number one item is usually Imodium, coming just above passport and airline tickets. No sooner had I returned to our hotel room after the dinner than I had to make an urgent dash to the bathroom. Not again! My mind flashed back to the traumas leading up to the Rio half marathon, which I so nearly had to pull out of and, in the end, completed in a lot of discomfort. Whether it was stress from race anxiety, the food I had just eaten, the water or the sudden change in temperature and climate, I just couldn't believe it was happening again. Why me?

To be fair, there wasn't the level of nausea I had felt in Brazil, but I did have to make a number of further visits to the bathroom during the night and, when the early-morning alarm call came to wake us, I informed Frank that I would give the sunrise visit a miss and focus on getting myself back to normal for the race, which was now only 24 hours away.

It proved to be a wise decision. A ten-kilometre hike around the base of Ayers Rock without a toilet in sight would have been memorable for all the wrong reasons and, happily, the stomach disturbance proved to be nowhere near as severe as the one I had endured in Brazil. By late morning, I was able to take another walk around Yulara on my own to visit some of the other lookout points.

The mandatory race briefing, at the resort's amphitheatre, was both thorough and entertaining. The red and yellow-shirted Travelling Fit team certainly knew how to choreograph what might otherwise have been a dull information-sharing session. Dozens of different countries were represented from every corner of the planet and, one by one, the athletes from each individual nation stood to the applause of others. Past winners were introduced, as well as some who had overcome major life challenges but would still make the start line. A representative of the local Aboriginal community gave an inspiring summary of his own running journey, and I even got to stand myself when it was announced that the most common birthday of all the competitors was 29 May! There were some serious safety presentations as well, and it was reassuring to hear from the chief of the local fire service that they considered the risk of wildfires to be zero, but that they would be out on the route in any case.

Hydration and medical support were available at the aid stations and route signage was then presented in theatrical fashion. Apart from the half and full marathon races, there were also shorter distances of 11k and 6k available, although these started later in the morning. The route markers for each event were colour-coded to hopefully keep everybody safe and on the correct track.

Armed with a headful of information and an abundance of good humour, we then headed for the pre-race carb-loading meal, which my stomach tolerated well, although I couldn't anywhere near match the size of the portions consumed by Frank. He seriously meant business the next morning.

* * * * *

It was a 5.30am alarm call and I had slept well. My stomach felt good; I was race ready. I'm not a great breakfast eater that early in the morning, but managed to wash down a banana and a croissant with some coffee. With dawn still some way off, I boarded one of the buses with Linda that would take us the relatively short distance out to the start/finish village. It was cold, very cold, and we were glad to have taken the advice to layer up, even though it would be getting very warm later. The bus took us as far as the Field of Light art display – an amazing installation of over 50,000 solar-powered flower stems, spread over an area the size of four football pitches, which soak up the daytime sunshine before lighting up at sunset and glowing throughout the night. As we arrived, the early red light of dawn was creeping over the horizon, so we never got to see it in its full splendour, but it was nevertheless a spectacular sight.

We walked to the race village, passing around the tables that would be laden with food for the end of our run. I took a bottle of water to sip from but, unusually for me, felt no need to join the queues for the portable toilets. For the run, I had again decided to wear my Camelbak, preferring my usual strategy of regular sips rather than large gulps every few miles at the aid stations. At one end of the field, two tall orange feather flags stood, bearing the name of the race, and we queued patiently for the opportunity to stand between them and have a souvenir photograph taken with Ayers Rock, glowing red in the early-morning sun, in the background.

The minutes ticked closer to the 7.30am start time and now it was time to get rid of those outer layers, leave our bags in a secure area and head for the inflatable starting arch. I wished Linda well. She was understandably nervous, this being her first half marathon for a number of years, and her sole intention was to finish it, regardless of time. Likewise, I had set myself no specific time target, largely because the nature of the course was such an unknown. As always, it was the experience rather than the time that I would judge the race by.

The deep, rich sound of a solo didgeridoo player echoed out across the landscape; it couldn't have been a more authentic Australian Outback setting. A comical moment. Over the loudspeaker, Michael, the race director, instructed us to line up at the starting arch, allowing the fast runners to be at the front and we lesser mortals behind. A few minutes later Michael came on again to tell us that, actually, we were all facing the wrong way; easy for the front runners who just had to spin round 180 degrees, but a longer trip for the backmarkers who now had to form a new queue in the opposite direction.

A loud and prolonged single note on the didgeridoo set us on our way. Overhead, a low-flying helicopter hovered, although the deep sound of the instrument could still be clearly heard above the noise of its rotors. Up ahead I saw Frank sprint away, already in second place behind a Kenyan runner. I started at a rather more measured pace and, after a sharp left turn out of the race village, encountered the soft red sand that would dominate at least 90 per cent of the route. It was not particularly deep sand but deep enough to drag on your trainers with each stride and to make me aware of the effort that this took.

The trail was relatively narrow but once the initial congestion in the first half mile had eased, it was wide enough to pass others and, indeed, be passed myself. I soon settled into what was a comfortable pace for me and, as the early-morning sun gradually began to climb, so did the temperature. The bushland around was much greener than I had expected. Hardy grasses and thorny bushes looked positively healthy in the seemingly parched soil. This was not how I expected the Outback to be. My mind had pictured shrivelled plant life, baked by the relentless sun and starved of water by drought conditions. We were to learn later that there had actually been six times the normal rainfall in the preceding year and this had led to this luscious abundance of plant life around us. One of the downsides of this was that both during the race, and our sightseeing tours afterwards, we would see very little of the animal wildlife that lives in this stark environment. When drought conditions dominate, they will congregate around human settlements in the hope of scrounging for food. When their surroundings offer a plentiful supply of nutrition, they will keep well away and there was certainly no shortage of space to hide in out here.

Another sharp right turn and there, maybe half a mile ahead of me on the straight red trail, the helicopter hovered perhaps only 100 feet above the ground, a yellow-suited crew member standing in the open doorway photographing the race unfolding below. What only became clear when we saw the final images was that this viewpoint gave them a dramatic perspective of the tiny runners toiling in the vast red desert with Ayers Rock looming in the background.

Our route then took us past the water treatment works for the town of Yulara, and this was not a pleasant experience. I held my breath for as long as I could but the wire perimeter fence seemed to go on forever and some degree of intake of the foul-smelling air was inevitable. I consoled myself with the fact that at least I was only running the half marathon, and that those poor souls running the full marathon would be encountering this section twice.

If I close my eyes now, many months after this run, what are my lasting impressions of running this race in the Australian Outback? Firstly, it was very flat; there were no significant hills. There was the occasional switchback mound but nothing of any note, although the dragging effect of the soft sand underfoot made this much tougher than a flat road race would have been. The other lasting memory was of how quiet it was out there, once the helicopter had disappeared, of course. There was birdlife around Yulara, including some striking crested pigeons, but once out in the wilderness, despite being surrounded by bushes and trees, just a deathly silence.

For ten increasingly warm kilometres, I ran non-stop, passing through the friendly aid stations as my Camelbak was meeting my hydration needs. Occasionally, the route would deviate on to a short section of tarmacked road before heading off into the bush again. At one of these junctions, the duty fire crew gave vociferous support as I passed, their truck ready for action but happily not needed. The low early-morning sun threw my long, dark shadow ahead of me, bringing back memories of a previous run in the Sahara when the then setting sun produced a shadow so impressive that I just had to stop and take a photo of it. I did so again on this occasion.

Although we seemed far away from anywhere, every now and again a random photographer would pop up from behind a bush to capture our expression of surprise. I even paused to take a couple of photos myself of particularly evocative views of the magnificent Ayers Rock, and also of the ten-mile distance marker, a reminder to the doubting voice in my head that I only had a 'parkrun' to go.

As I entered the final miles, I began to encounter other runners, some even racing in the opposite direction. Some of these were from the 6k and 11k races and I had to keep reminding myself to follow the black direction arrows at the junctions where the routes deviated. On a few occasions, I would meet an athlete with a red race number on their vest and would shout words of encouragement – these were the brave souls running the full marathon distance, essentially running the same loop again but in reverse.

Soon the race village came into view and, after miles of red sand and silence, the hubbub from the watching crowd began to grow. The camera had been put away now and I was running strongly. Suddenly those muscles that had felt so drained by the soft surface had renewed energy and the imminent prospect of completing a race on one more continent drove me on. A sharp left turn and then one final sprint around the perimeter of the race village, lined with the multi-coloured flags of all the nations taking part, the public address system calling out my name and then, arms outspread, I had done it. I sank down on to my haunches, gasping for breath from the exertions of that final sprint and, with the forefinger of my right hand, drew a little tick into the red soil.

There was no shortage of food available to quickly replenish the energy stores – fruit, sandwiches, muffins and hot dogs – but my appetite normally takes an hour or so to recover, so my intake was modest, although I hastily downed a bottle of cooled water. I wondered how Linda was getting on and walked back towards the long straight that led to that final lap. Before too long, I could see her unmistakeable running style in the distance. Regular runners will know that you can often identify a running friend by their unique style, long before you can see their faces. I stood at the sharp turn that led on to the perimeter lap and shouted encouragement. There was a brief smile, quickly replaced by sheer determination, and when Linda crossed that line, all the emotion of the journey she had been through over the past five years came out. Her goal had been achieved and I felt so proud of her.

It wasn't long before the tannoy announced that the leader of the full marathon was approaching the finish and, sure enough, it was my room-mate Frank. He absolutely sped around that final circuit and crossed the line just a few seconds under the three-hour mark, looking almost embarrassed by the attention he was receiving and, rather annoyingly, looking as fresh as a daisy. In contrast, the legs of the third-placed finisher buckled as he reached the line, and he was stretchered away for treatment; conditions were now getting brutal out there.

When the results finally came through, they confirmed that I had run my fastest 'wilderness' half marathon, even with a few photo stops. Even more confidence-building for me was my placing of 58th out of 171 runners in the half marathon, a much better performance than I would normally expect to achieve, although whether that was down to my fitness level or the quality of my fellow runners could be debated. Six continents down, one to go, and I still had it in me. As I sat on the bus that was taking us back to Yulara, I felt that inner warm glow that comes from a good run. For me, this was enhanced by the bus driver playing Pink Floyd's *Dark Side of the Moon* album at an extraordinarily loud volume – one of my favourites. Linda seemed less impressed.

After the exertions of the race, it would have been nice to think that I could relax and unwind for the rest of the day. However, before setting off for Australia, we had been given the chance to book some optional excursions, all of which had proved to be very popular, and the two I had chosen both fell on the day of the race. I even questioned the tour company to see whether it was possible to fit all this into one day, but was assured it was – just!

After a refreshing shower and a welcome change of clothing, I was picked up from the hotel by minibus for trip number one, a helicopter flight over Ayers Rock. I was only going to visit Ulura once in my life, so I might as well view it from every angle possible. We were taken out to the same airport we had flown into just a couple of days before, given a thorough safety briefing, and then I hopped on board the black and yellow aircraft, where I and three others were equipped with headphones and microphone to both hear from, and communicate with, the pilot.

Once airborne, the views were stunning. At every horizon, the land was flat, and this would be only a tiny portion of the Australian Outback but then, seemingly from nowhere, the orange sandstone mass that was Ayers Rock rose upwards. Just a few tiny patches of greenery were visible on the lower slopes, but above that bare rock scarred by channels formed by waterfalls when the heavy rains fell.

Around the base, vegetation was sparse and the ground looked barren and parched, but looking west towards the multiple domes of Kata Tjuta, trees and bushes were abundant, no doubt hiding some of the wildlife that had been concealed from our view. We circled the rock, viewing it from all sides before then getting a bird's eye view of Yulara, looking dwarfed in the vast open spaces, before making our way back to the airport.

No sooner was I back on the ground, and whisked back to the hotel, than it was time for my next excursion. This time I was going to see – yes, you've guessed it – Ayers Rock! Well, to be honest, if you are staying in Yulara, there isn't really very much choice unless you are prepared to travel for several hours, and this was a once-in-a-lifetime opportunity to watch the sun set over it.

By road this time, we were taken into the National Park itself and dropped off at a viewing point much closer to the rock. Here, there was a pleasant and unexpected surprise. Tables were laden with finger snacks, crisps and dips, not to mention a plentiful supply of water, orange juice, glasses of bubbly and red wine, all provided free of charge by the bus company that ran the tour. I may have passed on the water and orange juice. As the sun slid towards the horizon, Ayers Rock, separated from us by a vast meadow of straw-coloured grass, was still pale orange, but then as my glass began to empty, and occasionally magically replenish itself, the orange began to darken and then pass through progressive shades of red, then purple and finally a sombre brownish-grey as the final vestiges of light disappeared from the sky. It was indeed captivating, like watching a giant chameleon reinventing itself every few minutes; certainly a sight I will never forget.

Once back in Yulara, I headed for the final celebration of what had been a long, exhausting but memorable day; an informal celebration drink at the local pub at the Pioneer Hotel, on the far side of the resort. Linda and Frank were already there, celebrating with many of our new Australian friends and Tim, the hard-working and ultra-efficient Travelling Fit representative at our hotel. Having been out on my two outings, I was pretty eager for some hot food and joined Linda in the queue for a do-it-yourself barbecue. Being the carnivore that I am, I opted for the bush selection of kangaroo, crocodile tail and emu sausage, cooked to perfection by my good self (under the guidance of a local chef) and accompanied by plenty of bread, salad and, yes, a couple more glasses of wine. Just as had happened after the Big Five Marathon in 2012, the pounding of the disco music and the probable loosening of my natural inhibitions by the wine (I am definitely not a natural dancer) saw me boogying again with Linda before we wandered back together across the bush trail by torchlight. Living on the opposite side of the planet to each other is no barrier to having great running friends.

* * * * *

For now at least, the running was done, but I still had a couple more days to spend in the Outback before moving on to my next destination. The morning after the race, just a little fragile from the night before, I set off on another excursion, this time to Kata Tjuta. Now, I appreciate that I may be accused of being inconsistent here in using the Aboriginal name for this cluster of soaring rock domes, rather than the English name of The Olgas. I did, after all, insist on using the name Ayers Rock rather than Uluru, largely because the name of the noodle house in Yulara just wouldn't have been so amusing if I had stuck to the Aboriginal version. I hope by being even-handed I will be forgiven, but it is worthy of note that throughout my visit to Australia, there were plenty of reminders to respect the wishes, customs and beliefs of the indigenous people.

Shortly before arriving at Kata Tjuta itself, our bus paused to give its passengers a toilet break at a public facility. Nothing unusual there, but this was an Australian Outback facility that basically meant a very wide and very deep hole drilled into the ground. If you dropped your mobile phone into that toilet, there was no getting it back!

On arrival at Kata Tjuta, and the Valley of the Winds, named for very obvious reasons, our party was offered the option of a one-hour return walk to the Karu lookout or the much more strenuous and steep full-circuit walk that would take around three hours. Despite my climb to the top of Sydney Harbour Bridge still being fresh in the memory, inner doubts about unprotected drops led me to choose the former, although

I felt slightly guilty at not giving it a go. Both groups walked together to the Karu lookout across steep slopes and rocky rubble. From here, we could now pick out the individual, and quite separate, domes rather than seeing the whole formation as a joined-up cluster. These, we were informed, were conglomerate rocks: granite and basalt held together by a matrix of the red sandstone we were so familiar with from Ayers Rock. A view that repaid the challenges of the walk that led up to it.

At this point, our smaller party retraced our footsteps back to the bus whilst our more adventurous companions dropped down some steep steps towards the valleys and creek beds. With time on our hands, our driver, who doubled as a very informative tour guide, took us to the Walpa Gorge, Walpa being the local word meaning windy. Again, another wonderful steep-sided and gently-rising rocky trail through a narrow gorge that offered water and protection to both rare plant life and animals from the harsh realities of the desert scrubland surrounding it. The perfumed yellow flowers of a grove of spearwood shrubs reflected in the still waters of the pools and marked the point at which the trail ended. To go further would have meant trespassing on land sacred to the indigenous people. We turned back.

* * * * *

There was an outdoor celebration of our running achievements that evening. We had been warned that it would get chilly and to wear hat and gloves, but the party mood ensured that we were at least warm inside. After walking through a tunnel of high fives from the Travelling Fit team, we climbed to a viewing platform at the top of a sand dune and, as the sun went down once more, gave a sparkling wine toast to those who had put on such a fabulous event. After canapés of crocodile and kangaroo, we returned down to lamp-lit tables, enjoyed a bowl of warming soup and then feasted ourselves on a bush tucker buffet of lavish proportions, with wine, beer and even after-dinner port flowing freely. Overhead, the clear night sky sparkled brightly and, as we ate and shared stories with our new-found friends, the resident astronomer, with the aid of an extremely powerful laser beam, guided us through the constellations, galaxies and planets of the southern sky.

It was time to say goodbye to Linda at the end of the evening as she was returning to New Zealand the following morning, with a few days off work to recover from her epic and emotional run. For me, it would of course be a very short-lived goodbye as we were due to meet up again in her home country in just a week's time but for other friends, strong bonds had been formed in just a few days of adventure and promises to keep in touch would not be broken.

* * * * *

There was one final Outback excursion on our last full day, to Kings Canyon. From a map, the straight line distance between Yulara and the canyon didn't look too lengthy, but between the two lay Lake Amadeus, a massive salt lake, the crumbly surface of which struggled to support the weight of animals, let alone a road. For our bus to reach there on sealed roads required a long detour around the lake and a journey of almost four hours each way. Mile after mile of emptiness with just the occasional desert camel as the only sign of life, and the flat top of Mount Connor the only blemish on an otherwise level horizon.

A trek around Kings Canyon is not to be taken lightly and this was reinforced to us when we were asked to sign indemnity forms on the bus journey in. To even enter the Watarrka National Park, which includes the canyon, you had to show that you were carrying at least three litres of water and, during the summer months, entry was forbidden if the forecast temperature was 36°C or above. Happily, on this day, temperatures were well below that. As if the weather hazards weren't enough on their own, even in the toilet facilities at the entrance to the park, ominous signs above the wash hand basins warned that bees may live inside the taps.

Once again, we were offered the choice of two walks and, once again, the wimp within me opted for the easier option. The full canyon rim walk involved an arduous, steep, 500-step climb up to what was known locally as 'Heartbreak Hill' or, more dauntingly, 'Heart Attack Hill'. Once on the rim, hikers were warned never to venture closer than two metres from the sheer drop. Once again, my fear of unprotected heights led me to choose the easier option of a walk along the bottom of the gorge, alongside the dried-up Kings Creek. With buzzards and falcons hovering overhead, we were treated to some quite extraordinary layered geological features, gigantic termite mounds, and a cascade of rock and tree debris from the last time heavy rains had poured water through the creek. Parts of the vegetation had been scorched by wildfires and our guide told us of trees and bushes that have evolved with their regenerative features below the surface, so that when fire sweeps through and destroys all above the ground, the tree or bush could still revive itself. Nature is amazing.

One final highlight of that walk for me was our guide's deep knowledge of the sometimes strained and mistrusting relationship between Australia's indigenous population and the white people who had come to settle in the country. I learned so much from that man about the Aboriginal skills, culture and customs that may sadly be lost forever.

* * * * *

My time in the Outback was over, although never to be forgotten. The race I had travelled so far for was done and dusted, literally, but I still had another two weeks Down Under, with more running to come. I flew back to Sydney with Frank and, at the airport, we went our separate ways; one of the nicest and most unassuming characters I had ever met, and an awesome runner to boot.

Next stop Brisbane.

Chapter 10

Family, friends and farming sheep

My week or so in Brisbane was a chance to catch up with, and spend some quality time with, family members of whom I had seen very little since they emigrated from the UK way back in 1973. Following the tragic loss of their parents, their children, Lee and Nicky, had built new lives in Australia. Lee had married and had two teenage sons although, sadly, his marriage had ended recently and he was now living in an apartment on his own. Nicky and her husband, Dean, had also been living through difficult times after Dean had been diagnosed with a benign brain tumour, which had been successfully removed, although the long recuperation period had had a major impact on their gardening business.

Lee had kindly offered to pick me up from the airport and to put me up in his apartment for the duration of my stay. Rather like me, he had always enjoyed worldwide travel, particularly in his younger days, and I had met him on a couple of occasions when he came back to the UK to visit relatives and, for a short period, to work in London, although this had been quite some time ago. We usually exchanged Christmas cards and emails but it had been many years since I had seen a recent photograph of Lee, so I felt some surprise when this smiling, grey-haired man came bounding up to me at Brisbane Airport, with his hand outstretched. Fortunately, he had recognised me instantly.

Lee was a teacher at Brisbane Boys' College, an independent day and boarding school located not too far from his home in Indooroopilly, one of the western suburbs of the city. For most days of my stay, he would be working as normal during the daytime, but I had full access to his apartment from which I could explore the city by taking the train into the central business district and, of course, we could enjoy the evenings and weekend together.

As I mentioned previously, before leaving the UK I had explored the option of booking guided running tours in the city and the surrounding bushland, as I had done in Sydney, but had discounted these. I would find my own routes and one run I would definitely be doing was the South Bank parkrun on the Saturday of my visit. I had already made contact with the local organisers to let them know to expect me. Fingers crossed it wouldn't be the nail-biting near miss that my Sydney parkrun had turned out to be.

From the moment we met, Lee and I bonded very quickly. Yes, I know we were family, but we lived as far apart as could be and, until this time, had had very little real face-to-face time together. Life had dealt us many of the same cards: loss of both parents, much earlier in Lee's case, marriage breakdown and the impact on the children, forming new relationships, workplace stresses and the resulting effect of all this on our mental wellbeing. We were both prepared to be very open with each other and, as a result, learned a lot from each other to take forward.

My daytimes were largely spent discovering the city on foot. I took a train ride from Taringa station, the nearest to Lee's apartment, to Central station and, from there, it was a relatively short walk down to the river, around which many of the sightseeing attractions were located. Priority number one was to find both the start and finish of the South Bank parkrun and this was soon achieved, with only a few hundred yards separating the two. Lee had already offered to give me a lift to the start, so there weren't likely to be any last-minute travel problems this time. Over the following couple of days, I walked both banks of the river, learning as much as I could about the city as was possible during the short time available. Between the station and the river was the City Hall which, apart from being a magnificent building, housed the Museum of Brisbane, which detailed the social development and art of the city since its earliest days. On the South Bank was the Queensland Gallery of Modern Art, the highlight for me being an enormous bronzed sculpture of an elephant standing on its head, peering at a tiny water-rat. The significance of this was lost on me, but again it provided an elephant link to another of my running trips. The Queensland Museum could easily have taken up a whole day, but I restricted myself to the natural history of the state, from the pre historic creatures that roamed its plains to modern favourites like funnel web spiders and deadly snakes.

Of course, as a tourist, a ride on the Brisbane Wheel felt almost obligatory, although this differed from our own London Eye in that, instead of one very slow rotation, we were treated to a number of faster rotations, with different parts of the city being pointed out on each circuit. A contemplative hour, with a sandwich and a coffee, was spent in the beautiful and picturesque surrounds of the Nepalese Peace Pagoda, the only remaining exhibit from the 1988 World Expo held in Brisbane, and this was followed by a gentle stroll through the City Botanic Gardens, originally planted by convicts, but now containing many species the like of which I had never seen before.

As I left the gardens, and returned towards the rail station, I saw yet another wonderful building, a red-bricked heritage listed warehouse dating back to the late 19th century. My infantile sense of humour meant I just had to take a photo of it. In large letters on the upper central façade, its original owners were identified as 'Smellie & Co'.

Of course, during the evenings, Lee was around. On the first evening he drove me up to Mount Coot-tha, which was visible from his apartment balcony and gave a fantastic panoramic view of the city below by night. Lee was an excellent cook and provided some fine meals of salmon and steak, usually accompanied by my contribution of red wine, and on other evenings we ate out at his local, the Pig 'N' Whistle in Indooroopilly, in the sometimes raucous company of many of his expat friends. It was on one of those evenings that I first met up with Nicky and Dean. I hadn't seen Nicky since she was a small child when the family emigrated and, of course, I had never met Dean, but we all got on famously from the beginning. Indeed, on my final Sunday in Brisbane, Lee, Nicky and I spent a wonderful day walking around the stunning bush trails and waterfalls of Tamborine Mountain. As I have said many times before, I just love listening to the sounds of nature around me and this was an extra-special treat. The sharp whip-crack call of the eastern whipbird will remain long in my memory. If there is to be a next time here, I would love to run those trails.

There were a few other highlights of my Brisbane trip, including a visit to the world-famous Lone Pine Sanctuary, where Lee and I were able to wander around amongst koalas, kangaroos and other Australian wildlife. I also got to see my first-ever rugby union match when Lee's college took on some local rivals. Personally, I am much more of a fan of our round-ball football game, and openly admit to not understanding all of the intricacies of the rules, but I was suitably impressed by the speed and skills of the college boys, and the sheer physical size of some of the 14-year-olds was positively daunting.

But running is my passion and I had to find time to squeeze a couple of runs into what was a very full family holiday. In the absence of a running guide like Mick in Sydney, I set out on my own one morning from Lee's home, adopting my usual strategy when running in unknown territory of deciding a distance in advance, this time about six miles, running half of it in any direction wherever my fancy took me and then, hopefully, retracing my footsteps back to base.

Parts of Indooroopilly are hilly, extremely hilly, and although I took advantage of a fast downhill start, I knew I would have to pay for it at the end. My route took me past the ground of Taringa Rovers, a round-ball football team, and then into green parkland, populated with eucalyptus trees with cockatoos resting in the branches, and alongside a golf course where I often found myself sharing the footpath with bush turkeys. As I approached my turning point, the route began to climb to an esplanade high above the western stretches of the Brisbane River below. On this occasion, I had remembered all the twists and turns I had taken on the way out and was soon back in familiar territory, although that final climb back up to Lee's apartment was every bit as bad as I had feared.

Run number two was, of course, the South Bank parkrun. I already knew where the start and finish areas were and Lee, not a runner himself, had offered to drive me down there. Now, parkruns in most of the UK start at 9am, half an hour later in Scotland to cater for the darker mornings, and it had been something of a shock to the system to find the Sydney parkrun starting at 8am. In Brisbane it was even earlier, 7am, but with the route taking in both banks of the river through the central business district, which would become very busy with tourists later in the day, this was understandable, although I did question what effect this might have on numbers if 7am starts were the norm at home.

Lee dropped me off nearby and I made my way down to the start, immediately being reassured by the presence of parkrun teardrop banners placed strategically alongside the footpath. No danger of my being late for the start of this one. There were few people around, even fewer of those dressed for running, but I was very early. I had been in touch with a lady who was one of the local organisers before I left the UK to let her know I was coming, but she had messaged me a few days earlier to say that she was ill, but would let Gareth, the event director, know. As I waited, I chatted to a lady who was a regular parkrunner, but from another part of Australia, and this was to be her first Brisbane run. She too was surprised by the lack of people around.

Time moved on. A nervous-looking young man approached me and said that this would be his very first parkrun and did I have any advice. I advised him just to relax and enjoy it and warned him that parkrun was very addictive. A small group approached the start area, a few of them wearing high-vis vests; now this looked more official. They turned out to be a party of visually-impaired runners with their guides and we shared a few laughs and took a few photos as we waited. Five minutes to go and still only around two dozen people at the start line!

But then, seemingly from nowhere, they appeared; over 400 runners walking and jogging around a bend in the riverbank towards us. It turned out that the pre-race briefing was held at the finish area, rather than the start, as there was more room. There was no time now for any introductions; the countdown was starting us on our way.

Wearing the apricot-coloured T-shirt of my home Arrow Valley parkrun, I set off down the footpath, determined to do myself justice. After a loop around the entrance to the Queensland Maritime Museum, the route began to climb as we moved on to the Goodwill Bridge that would take us across to the north bank of the river. At about the midpoint of the bridge, a breathless male figure drew alongside me.

'Doug?' he exclaimed.

'That's me,' I replied.

'Gareth, event director.' We shook hands as we ran. 'I gave you a shout out at the briefing but didn't see your hand go up.'

I explained what had happened, and that I was waiting at the start.

'Look mate,' he went on, 'I can't keep up with this pace. Can we chat at the end?'

I gave a thumbs up and ran on. He was a younger man than me and that comment gave me a confidence boost.

Once over the bridge, we turned back down towards river level before following the riverside footpath past the central business district, passing under several bridges on the way, including the iconic Kurilpa Bridge, a unique and visually impressive structure of steel masts and cables at varying angles supporting the concrete deck slabs that carried pedestrians and bicycles across the waters.

As the river swung round to the left, we were approaching the Go-Between Bridge, named after the rock band who were formed in the city, and our route back across to the south bank. Here, there was a surprise in store as we had to climb a few flights of steps to get up on to the bridge, with a few flights down to get back off again. From there, with less than a mile to go, a mixture of tarmac path and wooden decking alongside the muddy banks of the river took us past the State Library, the Queensland Museum and ferry terminals to the finish area at Parklands. It had been a good run, about half a minute quicker than my run in Sydney, despite the flights of steps, and another international location ticked off for my parkrun portfolio.

There was one of those rather unusual quirks of fate following the run. I managed to locate Gareth once he had finished and, after a brief chat about our respective parkrun experiences, Lee, who had met me at the finish, took a photo of us both standing next to the parkrun Australia banner. I posted this photograph to Facebook and, just a short time later, my son, Chris, posted a picture of a Telford-based couple standing in exactly the same location. I recalled at the start that I did see a T-shirt in the familiar gold and green quarters of Telford Harriers, but, as over 10,000 miles separated the two places, I assumed that this was just a coincidence. How wrong can you be? Yes, parkrun shrinks the world, and as a timely aftermath, I was able to be introduced to the couple at Telford parkrun just three weeks later.

* * * * *

It was time to move on to the final leg of my trip Down Under and a visit to my running friends in New Zealand. Lee already had plans for a visit to his nan's in the UK later in the year and, as she lived barely 20 miles from me, I was happy to reciprocate his kindness and offer him accommodation whenever he needed it during his stay. With so much in common with our lives, we had bonded very closely during the week and it was reassuring to know we would be meeting up again soon.

* * * * *

It was an early start to catch the first flight of the day to Wellington in New Zealand and I received a pleasant, but probably unwarranted, surprise when I was presented with a lovely cooked breakfast of four pancakes with mango and peaches and a blueberry muffin, while all those sat around me on the plane looked jealously on, as they nibbled at their small packet of biscuits. Apparently, it had been pre-purchased for my seat number, although I had absolutely no recollection of doing so.

Apart from a tiny bit of rain on my final day in Brisbane, my visit to Australia had been wall-to-wall sunshine from day one in Sydney, so it was a bit of a wake-up moment to be flying over snow-peaked mountains as we descended into Wellington, although not entirely unexpected.

After having my trail running shoes washed by the customs officer to remove any remaining traces of the Australian Outback, I sat in the departure lounge to pass a few hours and wait for the next flight on to Invercargill. Overhead, and suspended from the ceiling, were three gigantic Harry Potter-esque eagles, one with a wizard riding on its neck, with huge talons reaching down towards the waiting passengers below. An unusual design feature, and one which caused a bit of alarm to some of the more fearful youngsters in the hall.

It was late afternoon and the light was fading as I finally sat aboard the Invercargill flight, after the inbound plane had been delayed. After the massive airliners of the trip so far, this was a much smaller craft, propeller-driven, and we waited patiently after the pilot informed us that one of the lights on the wing tip needed to be changed before we could take off. Despite several engineers toiling at the top of stepladders for some time, this proved to be a far more difficult job than simply changing a light bulb and soon we, along with our luggage, were being ushered off the plane to await a replacement. Fortunately, we didn't have long to wait.

* * * * *

Jan and Linda were waiting for me at the small airport in Invercargill. Of course, it had only been a week since I had been with Linda, but she wanted to be there to welcome me to New Zealand. Jan looked no different from when I had last seen her after our elephant escapade in South Africa five years earlier, but that cheery exterior hid the bad luck that seemed to follow her around as, like me, she took on running events around the world.

2017 had been an immensely challenging year for Jan and her sheep-farming husband, Andrew. Earlier in the year, Andrew had suddenly experienced extreme fatigue and breathlessness and had been diagnosed with endocarditis, a potentially fatal infection of the inner linings of the heart and, in Andrew's case, most probably picked up from his farming activities. One of his heart valves had been so badly damaged that it had had to be replaced by a cattle heart valve and for several days it was touch and go whether he would survive. Happily, he was now gradually recuperating.

I have already mentioned how extreme weather and hypothermia had scuppered Jan's dream of running a full marathon in Antarctica in 2016 although, being the lady she is, she had already rebooked a return visit to the White Continent.

Jan had also entered the 2017 Marathon des Sables (Mds), the 140-mile stage race I had run in 1999. Initially, she was unsure she could even go with Andrew being so ill but his recovery from open-heart surgery was progressing well and, in the end, they decided that she would take part.

Jan is a slower runner – she won't mind me saying that. In a race like the MdS, that means you are out there in the sun for much, much longer than the faster runners, and consequently, have less time to recover before the next stage begins. Jan completed the first three stages of around 20 miles each. She also completed the stage everybody fears the most: the 48-mile fourth stage. This left one final leg, a 26-mile marathon. Around halfway through that, Jan collapsed with heatstroke and extensive burns damage to her feet and legs, and was medically evacuated to a hospital in Casablanca.

In her own words, the next two weeks were probably the toughest of her life. While race organisers and insurance companies argued about who was liable for what, Jan was left alone in a hospital where the staff spoke very little English. In an Islamic society, the nursing staff were reluctant even to feed or bathe her without her husband being present.

'Where is your husband?' they constantly asked. Andrew was, of course, many thousands of miles away, still recuperating from his heart surgery. Finally, arrangements were agreed that would permit Jan to be flown back to New Zealand with a nurse, where she would spend a further two weeks in hospital in Dunedin.

Now, five months on, Jan was only just beginning to take her first tentative steps back into running, her legs and feet still carrying the scars of the desert.

* * * * *

After dropping Linda off at her car, Jan drove me out to their sheep farm in Wyndham. I must admit it was a lot further out from Invercargill than I had imagined, about a marathon's distance away in fact. The roads in the city were wide enough for a plane to land on but they were carrying very little traffic. Around 45 minutes later we arrived at Brook Farm, where a healthy-looking Andrew was waiting to greet us with a tasty late-evening snack of egg and tomato on toast, followed by a real treat of some Bluff oysters.

Andrew was a giant of a man but not a runner, unless angry elephants were around. We joked that one of the funnier lasting memories of the elephant chase was the sight of Andrew leading the hasty retreat from the charging beasts down into the ravine, leaving his poor wife, Jan, trailing in his wake. To this day, he insisted he was showing leadership.

Jan is a kindergarten teacher and so was at work during much of my stay but Andrew kept me busy, both helping him on the farm and, when he had a couple of hours to spare, taking me out on a few sightseeing trips. Any thoughts of a solo run around the surrounding countryside were soon scuppered as all the livestock had to be fenced in and the roads were very narrow, with huge logging lorries thundering up and down. That didn't mean I wouldn't get a run in, though!

✻ ✻ ✻ ✻ ✻

My first full day was very tiring but such great fun. It was lambing season and, for Andrew, that meant being available 24 hours a day to check on the ewes that were about to produce. Very early mornings, very late nights and for a man still recuperating from heart surgery, an enormous workload. Andrew also led a gang of shearers and was constantly on his phone making arrangements with sheep farmers in the district and beyond.

My first job with Andrew was to help move a whole flock of sheep down a country road and on to a new pasture. Easier said than done. My main task was to wave down traffic coming down the lane while Andrew urged them along with his truck. Inevitably, a few sheep turned back on themselves and I did my very best to keep them moving in the right direction. Basically, you have to make a lot of noise and wave your arms about.

After lunch, we moved the sheep into the sheds, where they were constrained within narrow-fenced passages. The new lambs had to be tailed and this was done by placing a tight rubber ring towards the top of the tail, which would restrict blood flow and, eventually, the tail would fall off, thus reducing the risk of infection arising from the full tail being so close to the lamb's back passage. Andrew gave me instructions on how to pick up and hold a lamb so that this could be done quickly and efficiently. I was learning fast.

The whole flock of lambs was then vaccinated by scratching to prevent a viral disease, given vitamin B12, and then the ewes and lambs were drenched by firing, from a gun-like probe, a measured dosage into their mouths to prevent internal parasites. Next, half of the flock had to be moved to another field some distance away and this involved separating them within the confines of the shed and then loading those that were moving on to a fenced-in trailer. Despite all the bleating and apparent chaos of sheep moving in every direction, the lambs still managed to find their own mothers.

It was beginning to dawn on me that there was much more to sheep farming than just putting them into a grassy field and letting them get on with it. This was reinforced the following morning when I joined Andrew at a sheep and beef farmer study day on a nearby farm. Sat on straw bales inside a barn, we listened to a Powerpoint presentation that contained a huge amount of science and mathematical modelling to determine the optimum conditions for raising livestock. We went out on to the hills during a break to learn how to assess the quality of the pasture, looking for the percentage of clover as well as grass.

Sadly, even though I have long been back in the UK, whenever I hike or run across a green field I still find myself assessing its quality for sheep farming. After lunch, a delicious giant burger and salad, we then spent a further hour with expert vets, learning how to assess the body condition of individual sheep.

If I could start my life all over again, I would never be a sheep farmer; it's too much like hard work and the hours are horrendous. If this was Andrew's workload when he was resting and recuperating from his operation, I can't imagine what his life must have been like when in full flow. Nevertheless, I thoroughly enjoyed my brief insight into Andrew's world. I guess it was the scientist within me that found it so captivating and it certainly ticked one of the boxes of activities that I'd never thought I would do in my life.

* * * * *

There was a pleasant surprise at the end of that first day on the farm when Jan phoned Andrew from work to say she was going for a run in the evening with the Southland trail runners from Athletics Invercargill. Would I like to join them? I didn't take too much persuading. Most of it would be in darkness so I borrowed a head torch from Andrew and he drove me towards Invercargill, where we met up with Jan, who took me to the start point at Sandy Beach.

Jan, of course, was still feeling her way back into running, so didn't feel up to the full 9k run planned, but would just do a short session on her own. There were seven of us who finally set off to run a route on twisting woodland trails, with plenty of steps to climb, both up and down. Most of the runners very soon disappeared off into the distance as they were a lot quicker than me, but the group leader, Glenn, kindly held back and we chatted all the way as we ran. Glenn was a very motivated and positively-minded competitor, so I pushed my pace a bit as I didn't want to slow him too much. He had only recently run under five minutes for a mile, so he was way out of my league, but we chatted about races past and present as well as more philosophical discussions on the impact that running had had on our respective lives. Glenn also had a running father, who was around my age, and I could sense that he was trying to work out who would win if his father and myself were ever to race together.

The chat and banter quickly passed the time and, after a steep section of stair climbing, we reached a high vantage point where the other runners had gathered to wait for us. Any remaining daylight had just about disappeared by now but looking out over the Foveaux Strait, we could pick out a few lights on Stewart Island, New Zealand's third largest. We set off again, this time with lots of descending through the wooded trails, and the head torch really came into its own as we twisted and turned between tree trunks and bushes in the gloom. Finally, we rejoined the path we had taken from Sandy Beach and the last two miles were much flatter and more open. I could feel Glenn was picking up the pace gradually; was he trying to test me? Of course, he could have left me for dust if he really wanted to, but I was determined to hang on in there and the final couple of miles were definitely the fastest.

I had that warm feeling inside that you get when you have pushed yourself as we finished, and were greeted by Jan and the rest of the team. It had been a good workout and I felt that I had needed it, as I had fewer running days in my legs than I would normally have done at home during the course of a week. And there was one final, but very welcome, surprise for the evening. One of the runners had arrived in his camper van and it was tradition that this was turned into a mobile pub at the end of the session. I had never met these guys before, and probably wouldn't again, but the shared experience of a night trail run on foreign soil led to a lively hour of jokes and laughter over a bottle or two of beer.

* * * * *

Despite his busy schedule, Andrew still found time to take me on a couple of sightseeing trips. With a bit of time on our hands following the farmers' study day, he had driven me to Curio Bay, the site of an incredible petrified forest, flattened by floods and volcanic debris 180 million years ago. It was also the home of some very rare yellow-eyed penguins, although they did not put in an appearance during our brief stay there. We moved on to Waikawa, a former fishing village with a cosy little museum showing the history of the area from the days of the early whalers, gold miners, saw millers and stone quarriers. Some of the early manual farm machinery had to be seen to be believed; you would need to be an immensely powerful person just to be able to use it.

Then there was Dunedin. Andrew had an early-morning medical appointment in the city, which was some two to three hours' drive away. We set off in his truck long before dawn, and paused on the way to check for new lambs on one of his pastures. This involved driving the truck, at some speed, in the dark around a hilly field, zig-zagging between bushes and trees, with the headlights picking out the sheep.

Bang! The truck hit an unexpected pothole and we were both launched into the air like rag dolls. Happily, the seat belts did their job and there were no after-effects other than a few hours of headache.

Once Andrew's appointment was over, we spent the rest of that day exploring parts of the city, with its very rich Scottish heritage marked by a statue of Robert Burns and several Scottish whisky bars. The railway station building was spectacularly magnificent, and that is not an exaggeration. It housed the New Zealand Sports Hall of Fame where I met John, Jan's father, who was now in his eighties, but who wouldn't know what to do with his time if he retired, so continues to work as a warden of the museum. We spent time in the Toitu Otago Settlers Museum, tracing the history of the Otago region back centuries to the Maori people, and the more recent 19th-century settlers from Europe, and indeed from China. In fact, just outside of the museum was a splendid Chinese Garden, one of very few outside China itself, and built to commemorate the contribution of the Chinese people to the history and culture of the city. So much to see and so little time to see it. A city to which I would certainly love to return.

* * * * *

So Linda, Jan and myself, with Andrew in support, were together once again and, despite all of the health problems of the intervening years, it would have been rude for us not to run together once more. Fortunately, Linda and Jan had identified a suitable race in the local running calendar, although it did require a long night-time drive into the mountainous Otago region and an overnight motel stay. Linda and I would enter the 10k race, between the towns of Clyde and Alexandra, while Jan opted for the shorter 6k distance as her very first race since her Saharan misadventure.

Our motel was in Alexandra, where the race would finish, and it was only in the morning that I could first see the beauty of our surroundings that had been shrouded in darkness on the drive in the night before. In stark contrast to the hustle and bustle of the cities of Sydney and Brisbane under warm winter sunshine, and the heat and eerie silence of the Outback, this was a small town surrounded by snow-capped mountains and noticeably colder than anywhere I had been in the previous weeks, including Invercargill.

As we waited for the bus that would be taking us to our respective start lines, the sun broke through the clouds and for a while its pleasant warmth left me with a brief dilemma. Whatever I was wearing to the start would be what I would have to run in, as there was no facility for transporting clothing left at the start back to the finish area. Did I need to wear my light windproof and waterproof jacket? In the end, I opted to keep it on – I could always tie it around my waist if I got too warm.

Thank goodness I made that decision. When the bus dropped us off at the stunning Clyde Dam, a viciously cold wind was howling down the valley. We were hopelessly exposed to it, the only shelter being a short, three-foot high brick wall along one side of a car park. Cue a busload of runners sitting and cowering on the ground trying not to leave any part of their bodies exposed above that wall.

And there was worse. An essential component of any race setting is the pre-race toilet facilities. At the top of Clyde Dam, three green portaloos stood swaying in the gusting wind. Just yards away, the ground fell away to the River Clutha far below. I ventured inside and the cubicle rocked violently backwards and forwards as I did the necessary. What a way to go that would be – trapped inside a flying portaloo on a 300-foot downward journey.

Soon, we were called to the start, which was at the opposite end of the top of the dam wall. Upstream, the waters of Lake Dunstan appeared to be boiling, the surface covered in a bubbling white froth whipped up by the wind. Far below, on the other side, the River Clutha flowed silently. I wished Linda the best of luck on yet another test of her growing recovery and then we were on our way, starting by re-crossing the dam with the wind threatening to rip the pinned number off my running vest. I clung to it tightly.

Once across the dam, the road immediately began to descend towards the town of Clyde, and with each advancing footstep the wind began to subside. Now I could really begin to take in the beautiful scenery we were running through: snow-capped mountains and pine forests all around, such a contrast to the heat and sand of the Outback just two weeks earlier.

The route itself continued alongside unremarkable, but quite busy roads. I was feeling strong. The long downhill from the start had meant that, once across the dam, I was running at a good pace for me and, for a while, a glance at my watch suggested I might even get close to the magic sub-50 minutes that I hadn't achieved for several years. In the final third of the race, as the road climbed back towards Alexandra, that particular dream disappeared, but I was still delighted to have recorded my fastest 10k of the year in challenging conditions.

At the finish line, I was greeted by Jan. Her 6k race had started half an hour before ours and she was so thrilled to report that she had managed to run every step of the way without any walking. She was on the comeback trail once again, and together we waited for Linda to come in, cheering as she beamed from ear to ear having comfortably beaten the time she had expected to finish in.

The grins in our post-race photos tell their own story. Friends who, despite their geographical separation, will forever share an unbreakable bond formed by those scary few minutes in Africa; each having set themselves a goal and not only reaching it, but surpassing it, and now all together once again. Yet another reason I love running.

* * * * *

And so it came to an end. Four very different weeks in four amazing locations. Whilst my passion for running was the glue that held it all together, there had been so many other highlights as well. Friends from the past and new friendships to take into the future. Family links strengthened and a stock of memories never to be forgotten. I actually felt quite emotional that it was all over.

I'm not a deeply religious person, but I am a believer. In times of real strife, I do find myself praying for guidance. My final day in New Zealand was a Sunday and it seemed right to join my friends at the Wyndham Evangelical Church to give thanks for the amazing adventures I had experienced during the previous month. And when, some two days later, I finally put my key into my own front door after the countless hours of flying home, Nougat was just fine.

Chapter 11

Three score years and ten

I took some time coming back to earth after my trip Down Under. It had been, by far, my longest stay away from home for any running adventure, or even holiday for that matter. There were family to catch up with and, of course, to share some of the countless photos I had taken during the four very different stages of my trip. I enjoyed a wonderful week when my sister, Lin, came to visit me from her home in Sussex and this included one of my all-time favourite parkruns at our local Arrow Valley event. Lin was a marathon runner with two 26.2-mile races to her credit, one being the London Marathon. But that was 30 years ago and it is fair to say that she hadn't been hooked on distance running since, in the same way that I had been. In fact, she hadn't done any sort of running since. A few years before, Lin had come to stay with me and I had dragged her along to our parkrun on a Saturday morning to soak up the wonderful atmosphere in her supportive spectator role. This time Lin wanted to run/walk it! We registered her for her barcode and both wore our coveted, individualised 'I Ran London' T-shirts. These were produced to commemorate the one-million plus finishers of the London Marathon, with number 1 being the winner of the inaugural event in 1981 (although it was a dead heat) and then increasing by one as each finisher crossed the line in subsequent years. My 1984 finish earned me number 49877 and Lin's finish three years later was rewarded with number 105991. We ran and walked around the parkrun course together, along with my ever-supportive friend, Julie, and although it was one of my slower times, it was also one of my more memorable parkruns; it is not the time that matters but the company that you are sharing it with, and that I think is the ethos of parkrun.

I got some miles back into my legs with two respectable half marathon times, one being in the nearby city of Worcester, and the other in the picturesque surroundings of Blenheim Palace, the birthplace of Sir Winston Churchill, in the Oxfordshire countryside. In November, Lee made his promised visit from Brisbane and we were again able to spend some quality time together as I returned his hospitality, at least in part. A new year was approaching and, for me, a highly significant one.

Whatever the future held, 2018 was going to be a landmark year for me. It would be the year in which I reached my 70th birthday. Three score years and ten. As a child, I can remember being taught that that was my likely lifespan. Of course, it seemed like an eternity then and I gained further reassurance when all four of my grandparents lived well beyond it. Sadly, my own parents fell some way short and that just reaffirmed that nothing in life was guaranteed, time was precious, and I vowed to squeeze as much as possible into the time given to me. I have been blessed with reasonable physical fitness, maybe not quite as strong in the mental health department, and certainly the latter half of my life has seen me make the most of my passion for running here, there and everywhere.

As I looked forward to the running year ahead, I did so in the knowledge that there were no guarantees against injury, illness or worse, but a plan had been set in place and I would do my very best to achieve it and, if I did so, I would have accomplished many of my personal goals by the time I completed my seventh decade.

The year began with a different sort of challenge, but one that was very meaningful and relevant to me. The mental health charity, Mind, was launching a fundraising campaign called 'Run Every Day January', shortened to 'RED January', which not only raised awareness of mental wellbeing issues but also reinforced the positive benefits of exercise on one's mental state. There were no minimum distance requirements and walking each day was just fine, but I set myself a goal of running at least five kilometres per day and, in doing so, broke my own rules. As a run leader, I would advise beginners to try to fit three sessions a week into their busy lifestyles in order to reap the benefits of regular exercise. For more experienced runners, whose bodies have adapted to the rigours of regular training – and I would include myself in that category – I would still advise one, maybe two, rest days a week in order to prevent overuse injuries. Rest days should definitely be considered to be part of a training regime, rather than simply a day off. Now, I was committing myself to 31 days of consecutive running. Was I risking injury in the lead-up to what promised to be one of the most exciting and challenging running adventures in my life; my long-awaited trip to Antarctica? I was prepared to at least give it my best shot and pledged 25p to the charity for every mile that I completed.

To cut a long story short, I did it. I won't pretend there weren't days when the cold and miserable winter weather had me looking for any excuse to stay indoors. Surfaces were often slippery with frost and I ran with caution to avoid any unwanted tumbles. As the end of the month approached, I began to question my own thoughts about rest days. I was actually feeling stronger than I had for a long time and my physical performance actually seemed to be benefitting from this extended run streak. On the 30th of the month, I completed a ten-mile run that included several personal records on particular segments of the route but then, back down to earth, I woke the next morning with a painful and swollen ankle.

There was no way I was going to stop now with just one day to go and so, with the aid of ibuprofen and a tight ankle strapping, I jogged gently around our five-kilometre parkrun route on the final day of the month. It was mission accomplished. Just over 165 miles of running in the calendar month, an average of five miles each and every day. Yes, I had done those sort of distances in the past, but never so many consecutive days. It made me feel good about myself and that was what the RED challenge was all about anyway. I may have been approaching the twilight years of my running career, and there is no way I am thinking of cutting back anytime soon, at least not voluntarily, but this was a different type of running challenge, and one which I had successfully completed.

Happily, the ankle injury proved to be very short-lived; the tried and tested RICE treatment (rest, ice, compression and elevation) had me back to a normal running regime within a week. It did serve as a warning, though, so I am now convinced that one or two rest days a week is sound advice after all.

* * * * *

Of the many runs I undertook in January, the one on the 27th will stay long in the memory. Without a shadow of a doubt, parkrun has changed my life. Since I ran my very first around my local lake at Arrow Valley, shortly after returning from our elephant escapade in South Africa, Saturday mornings have seemed incomplete unless started with a parkrun. Of course I have missed some due to important family events, through illness or injury and even taking my turn at volunteering, an essential and rewarding feature of a parkrunner's life. Even when away from home for a weekend, there is nearly always a local parkrun to join. Indeed, both Sydney and Brisbane had already allowed me to open my international parkrun tourist account.

I have made hundreds of new friends through parkrun, and that is no exaggeration. It has led me into the pathway of becoming a run leader and passing on my experience and knowledge to others, particularly those starting out on their own running journey. My own tribulations with mental health issues, and the benefits I have gained from being a runner and part of a supportive parkrun community, also led me to becoming a Mental Health Ambassador for England Athletics and to hold a similar role with the wider parkrun community, to help others who might find themselves in similar situations.

One feature of parkrun that rewards its participants and volunteers is the milestone T-shirts, presented free when you reach a certain level of achievement. White for juniors who have completed ten parkruns, and lilac for the hardy volunteers who may have stood out in the rain and cold on 25 occasions, but without whom parkrun could not exist. The red and black T-shirts, which mark the completion of 50 and 100 runs respectively, hang proudly in my wardrobe, and on 27 January I reached the 250 parkruns milestone that would qualify me to wear the coveted olive green T-shirt.

It was a memorable morning in so many respects and even the rainy weather didn't dampen our enthusiasm. To close friends and family, who wanted to dress up to mark the occasion, I had suggested a theme of 'Running Hot & Cold', and I opted for the hot end of that spectrum by wearing the very same T-shirt, race number and desert cap I had worn when racing 140 miles across the Sahara back in 1999. The T-shirt had been hung in my wardrobe ever since, a sort of trophy of the event. It had been washed, you will be pleased to hear, but still bore many sand-coloured stains from its previous outing. For those wondering whether I wore the original pair of shorts, they had long been consigned to a landfill fate!

In keeping with the theme, my son Chris combined both extremes by wearing a ski helmet and goggles with Bermuda shorts, Phillipa opted for a snowman outfit and Julie braved the January weather by running in a bikini, although with the sensible precaution of thermal layers beneath! The family group was completed with Chris's wife, Lynne, and my lovely grand-daughter, Holly, now 11 years old. I have run several times with Holly and I will never grow tired of it. As the title of this book suggests, there need be no age barriers to running together. I remember the pride I felt when I first ran with my own children many years ago; that delight seems to be magnified to an even greater extent when it is your grandchildren you are running alongside.

Unbeknown to me, a number of my fellow parkrunners were running in laminated 'Doug' masks to mark the occasion, prepared from a photograph of me competing in the Australian Outback – such a warm feeling being part of such a friendly and humorous community.

We laughed for every step of the five-kilometetre run, with Holly powering away from us on her young legs from time to time, and in the café afterwards I was presented with a giant chocolate cake commemorating my landmark run, which I was happy to share with all those present.

Also receiving a cake on that morning was another friend, Hayley. This was to recognise her 50th parkrun, but that tells only a tiny part of her story. Hayley worked in sports development for our local council and Arrow Valley parkrun was her brainchild back in 2012. You may think that 50 parkruns in over five years was no great achievement, but Hayley rarely got to run herself as she was involved in so many successful community projects. It was Hayley who put me on the path to becoming a run leader and she was the force behind the numerous Couch to 5k courses that have run in our town of Redditch since.

It hadn't all been plain sailing for her; two new parkruns launched within the district proved not to be sustainable because of local issues but our Saturday morning parkrun at Arrow Valley, which once hosted just 12 runners on a snowy January morning in 2013, now saw over 400 join in every single week. And Hayley's remit didn't stop at parkrun. The town now has a thriving triathlon club, two new, growing running clubs and various other sporting initiatives for young and old to help everyone lead healthier and, hopefully, happier lifestyles. I have a lot to be grateful to Hayley for.

* * * * *

Thoughts now turned to perhaps one of the most exciting challenges I had ever faced. It had been three years since I had paid my initial entry deposit for the 2018 Antarctica half marathon to mark the year of my 70th birthday and, in that time, it had been filed away in the back of my mind as one for the future. Of course, it had come to the forefront for that very brief period in 2016 when I was offered a last-minute place after somebody dropped out, but with the health issues I was suffering at the time, I am happy I stayed with my original plan. Now that I had successfully completed my runs in Rio and in the Outback, Antarctica now had the added significance of potentially being my seventh and final continent. I registered my previous achievements with the Seven Continents Club and, after they were all verified, I knew that if I crossed the finish line in Antarctica I would be one of very few people who had achieved half or full marathons on each of the seven continents.

There was some disappointing news, too. My doctor friend, Alma, who had been on the Myanmar and Rio running adventures, had also booked a place in Antarctica in her own quest for running a full marathon on all of the continents. Alma, a far more gifted runner than me, having won the ladies' marathon in Myanmar, would also have been celebrating a decade milestone birthday during the trip itself, although not as many decades as I had under my belt. However, since our last meeting in Rio, Alma had suffered a catastrophic injury to her kneecap and, despite a variety of treatments and keyhole surgery, had reluctantly had to withdraw from the race. Understandably, she was heartbroken. I shared her disappointment and hope that one day we do get to run together again; her kindness and support when I was ill in Rio will not be forgotten.

As the weeks ticked by, the reality of what I was about to face began to dawn on me. It was not the running of a half marathon that daunted me; for goodness sake, I had done enough of those. It was not the cold that concerned me. I have already run half marathons in wintry conditions in Siberia and on the Arctic ice cap in Greenland. I guess it must have been the sheer remoteness and unpredictability of Antarctica; like no other place on this planet. With the knowledge of how my anxiety levels had soared in the lead-up to my run in Greenland, I had to keep things in perspective. Souls far braver than myself had pitted themselves against the continent's extreme elements and hauled heavy sleds laden with supplies and dragged them to the very South Pole. My own dear friend, Miles, the blind runner who I ran with in the Sahara and in Siberia, came within 300 miles of the pole himself before having to be evacuated because of frostbite, and of course his guide, Jon, made it all the way to plant the flag of the Royal National Institute of the Blind at our world's most southern extremity.

My adventure would be very different. The run would take place on the remote King George Island, home to a handful of international research stations. We would not be hauling our supplies but would be running in conditions so unpredictable and potentially dangerous that there could be no guarantees that the event would even take place. It could be a completely wasted journey if Mother Nature decided to show her darker side. Getting to the start line would be an adventure in itself. For two days, we would travel by sea in a Russian ship from Ushuaia on the southern tip of Chile across the Drake Passage, a sea renowned by sailors for centuries for the intensity of its storms because of the temperature contrast between the ice and the converging open Atlantic, Pacific and Southern Oceans. It is the only part of the planet where sea completely encircles the globe so there is no land interface to calm the stormy seas. Even on arrival in Antarctica, there would be no accessible jetty for the ship to moor up to. It would have to drop anchor offshore, and landing on the continent would be accomplished by means of inflatable zodiac boats with small outboard engines. For a non-swimmer, that causes a little trepidation.

But the potential rewards were so great. Only a tiny, tiny percentage of human beings would ever get to see the Antarctic continent with their own eyes in their lifetime, and experience both the beauty and hostility of this unique part of the planet. Even fewer would ever get to set foot on it. The opportunity to come face to face with the living creatures that have evolved to live in this most inhospitable of environments was one that comes to few, and I was looking forward to it with a mixture of excitement and fear.

* * * * *

As with any foreign running adventure, preparation was key, and Marathon Tours, who were the organisers of the race and the trip, excelled in providing information and race briefings on matters that were unique to this part of the world. Clothing for the race I was fairly comfortable with; I had built up a collection of cold weather running gear that could deal with just about any eventuality weather-wise after my previous trips to Greenland and Siberia. What about footwear? The advice given to us was that ordinary trail shoes would suffice as the race route was on trails between the research stations and, in previous years, mud from the impact of global warming on the glaciers had been the major problem. I was unconvinced. It was unlikely that I would need anything as drastic as the crampon-like spikes I had pulled over my running shoes on the mile-thick ice cap of Greenland. Anything less than that on the ice cap would have been an accident waiting to happen, but they did add considerable weight to my shoes. Nevertheless, I packed them just in case. I also took along some metal-studded overshoes that I had found to give good grip at home in conditions where ice was very shallow. Both the size and weight of the single item of luggage allowed on the trip were relatively limited, so it was with some relief that I heard I wouldn't need to take my bulky down-hooded jacket, which had served so well in Siberia, as we would be provided with these on the ship for shore landings.

For hydration, I planned to use my Camelbak. This had an insulated drink tube to stop the water from freezing and would allow me to keep to my regular strategy of frequent sips rather than gulping larger volumes of water every few miles. We would be entirely self-sufficient for the race itself, so there would be no convenient drink stations manned by volunteers, but the likely repeated-loop nature of the route lent itself to runners leaving numbered water bottles at designated points if they so wished.

I also like to use energy gels for nutrition on any run beyond ten miles, so was rather taken aback when it was announced, in one of the briefings, that sachets of these would not be allowed on shore. The understandable reason for this was that the foil wrappers were very likely to be blown away by the very strong winds for which Antarctica had a reputation. In such a pristine environment, we had been reminded time and time again that the only thing we would be leaving behind in Antarctica would be our footprints. Once again, the problem was easily solved with a little online research, and I bought a soft, flexible bottle that could hold up to four gels, with a bite valve that would allow me to take just as much as I needed at the time. Not only would this deal with the foil wrapper problem, but it was a much more efficient solution for all my future events where I needed to carry gels, replacing the gel belt where the sharp corners of the foil wrappers are often caught on your swinging arms as you run.

Photography was another issue. I was only going to visit Antarctica once in my life and wanted to capture as many images as I could of what promised to be a unique experience. Ideally, I would have taken my digital single lens reflex camera, with a selection of lenses, so that I could catch the wider landscapes as well as close-ups of the wildlife. This had two problems: firstly, the weight of the equipment and, secondly, the prospect of damaging expensive items in the harsh and potentially very wet conditions on board the zodiacs. In the end, I opted to buy a lightweight point and shoot camera that was both shockproof and waterproof; I would always have my phone as a back-up, although this had very limited storage capacity.

However, no matter how much there was to think about in terms of packing everything I would need for the run, my major worry was not about surviving the Antarctic climate but the sea journey getting there.

I have never taken a holiday sea cruise. I have undertaken a number of short ferry journeys across relatively narrow expanses of water, but one prolonged sea journey remains as fresh in my mind today as it did when it happened more than 60 years ago.

It was a family holiday to the Channel Islands travelling on the ferry from Portsmouth. The seas across the English Channel were rough – very, very rough – and I, along with the vast majority of passengers as I remember, was very seasick. There was vomit everywhere in the corridors and lounges of the ship and the stench only exacerbated the problem. To make matters worse, the sea conditions were so bad that we were unable to enter the port at our destination and had to ride out the storm outside the shelter of the harbour walls. I just remember feeling that I was in an utterly hopeless situation and that I would never feel better again. Of course, once we finally reached dry land, I recovered very quickly but the recollection of that experience has meant that I have avoided prolonged sea travel ever since. How, then, would I cope with the Drake Passage?

The advice from Marathon Tours, who were clearly aware that this could be a significant problem if the Drake Passage lived up to its reputation, was to take a good supply of Dramamine tablets, but these were not available in the UK. My pharmacist was concerned that some of his over-the-counter remedies for travel sickness might interact with the prescription medicines I was already taking. In the end, I took a triple-pronged approach to the potential trip-spoiler. My GP prescribed me some hyoscine patches, which could be placed behind one ear, with each patch being effective for three days. I was advised to wear one before I even left home just to make sure that there were no unpleasant interactions with my other medications. Secondly, I purchased a pair of acupuncture wrist bands to be worn for the entire ten-day duration of the sailing, and finally, I crossed my fingers very tightly and prayed I would not have to endure a sea journey similar to that one of my childhood.

* * * * *

And so, the final few weeks turned into the final few days. I packed and repacked my bag, checking and rechecking I hadn't forgotten something of vital importance, and ensuring it stayed within the weight limit that was dictated by the airlines and the size limit imposed by cabin space on the ship. Reassuringly, my anxiety levels remained well under control in contrast to the lead-up to some of my previous trips. That was until the last couple of days before departure when that tiresome inner voice started to question why I repeatedly put myself into these situations, but there was no turning back now.

Chapter 12

Bake, lake and shake

Although the nerves began to settle as soon as I was on my way to Heathrow for my late-evening flight, the forgetfulness that perhaps is inevitably part of later life had me constantly checking pockets and travel wallets to make sure I still had all the vital documents with me. My inner fears were soon realised. Having checked my bag in and successfully negotiated the security queues at the airport, a cold chill went down my spine when I suddenly realised I must have left a plastic folder containing vital car parking and race documents in my luggage trolley. For goodness sake, I still had over 8,500 miles to travel to my final destination and I couldn't even get away from my departure airport without losing something! Happily, a radio call back to landside soon had me and my precious folder reunited, but it was a timely reminder.

Boarding was no easy matter, either. First the crew had been delayed in arriving by unexpected rush-hour traffic travelling from central London. Unexpected? Really! Then there was a last-minute aircraft change; not a problem in itself but this time it was a change to a different type of aircraft altogether, with a completely different seating configuration. Cue a lot of unhappy people, who had previously been sitting close to each other but were now separated. After some careful swapping negotiations, we were finally allowed to board. I still retained my aisle seat but was much further forward than my original seat had been. As soon as I settled into my place, my heart sank. Now don't get me wrong, I've been a parent who has flown with small children and I've felt that terrible guilt when they just won't settle and start to cry and even scream. The couple in the row in front of me had not one, not two, but three infants: twin babies about six months old and a young boy aged about two or three. Facing a 14-hour-plus night flight, this could all have got very messy.

There was what I can only describe as some adult female wailing from the rear of the cabin shortly after take-off, but it soon stopped and I put it down to someone struggling with a fear of flying. A glass or two of red wine and a very tasty dinner and I settled back to get what sleep I could. It's never comfortable on a flight that long in the rear cabin, cramped and chilly, but I was getting more sleep than I expected and the youngsters in front slept relentlessly, only being woken for an occasional feed.

In fact, when we finally landed in Buenos Aires, not a tear had been shed between the three of them, and I take my hat off to the parents, who must have felt triumphant. Unfortunately, the same couldn't be said about the wailing and sobbing from behind and for about the last hour of the flight, this grew in intensity. Having a few phobias myself, I felt some degree of sympathy with the lady but her behaviour was becoming more and more extreme, and obviously causing concern to the cabin crew. She was removed to the rear kitchen space, but this only prompted screams of 'get your hands off me!' and 'leave me alone!' It can't be easy being cabin crew under that sort of pressure.

After landing and waiting patiently in line for immigration, the wailing started again. What! We were on land now, but for the first time I could see the instigator. This was no case of a flying phobia as I had wrongly assumed; this was a young lady falling out with her male partner, who looked hideously embarrassed himself, as she screamed, sobbed and stomped her way along the queue. In future, I'll take a plane full of babies any time!

* * * * *

I had not been the most popular person in my local running community over the weeks leading up to departure. The previous autumn, I had made it publicly known that I was hoping for a really cold winter to help me to prepare for my Antarctic adventure and to test out my equipment choices. My prayers had been answered in the most emphatic fashion possible, and the cold, icy and occasionally snowy days had continued long into the time that we would have liked to have called spring. I took the blame for this and, indeed, when I left the UK, my body was indeed fully adapted to running in icy conditions.

What I hadn't really taken into account was just how hot it would be in Buenos Aires, our stopping-off point on the journey south. As soon as I stepped off the aircraft, it was as though I had opened an oven door and this was in the early-morning hours. I was going to have to adapt to running in these steamy conditions before being plunged back into the cold in a few days' time.

With competitors flying in from all over the world, there were several Marathon Tours staff at the airport to greet us and take us on to our hotel base in the city, which proved to be very well appointed indeed. It was while waiting at the airport that I first got chatting to Rupert, a fellow Brit from London. He had been on the same flight as me, although neither of us was to know that at the time. He had also been seated much closer to the wailing lady, so had his own different perspective of the final hour of that flight. Despite the considerable age gap – Rupert was only 30 – we got on well from the beginning, so it was good to know when we checked in at the hotel that he would be my room-mate for the three nights we would be spending in Buenos Aires before heading further south.

After a getting-to-know-you lunch with Rupert alongside the waterfront, we returned to the hotel, got changed into very lightweight running gear and gathered in the lobby for a group run. The temperature outside was over 30°C; I was certainly not expecting to run in such heat on this trip!

If I had had any concerns about not knowing anybody on this trip once Alma had withdrawn, these would soon be alleviated. A friendly lady came bounding up to me as we waited and said she recognised me from Rio de Janeiro. Cindy began to relate the story of how we spoke after a similar group run in that city, when she noticed me wearing my personalised 'I Ran London' T-shirt that I mentioned previously. The penny dropped; of course I remembered the occasion. Soon we were joined by Sheri, who had also been in Rio. They too now possessed their own personalised London T-shirts and wanted to thank me for pointing them in the right direction. Both ladies were now on the brink of their own seven continents achievement, but at the even more awesome full marathon level. We were to spend a lot of time together on the trip, along with Cindy's husband, Larry, who would not be running but would nevertheless play a vital role when the race unfolded.

Around 30 of us set off for the run, which took us around a beautiful ecological reserve and past bronze statues of famous Argentinian sportsmen and women, including Lionel Messi, Juan Fangio, Roberto di Vicenzo, Guillermo Villas and Gabriela Sabatini. With the oppressive heat, I opted for a shorter five-kilometre loop that included a spectacular viewpoint over the Southern Atlantic Ocean, which just couldn't be ignored and provided a brief mid-run respite from the tough conditions. Once again, my ears were tuned to the bird sounds, with several being unique to this part of the world. Others, mainly the full marathon runners, opted for a longer nine-kilometre loop through the same reserve, but with tired bodies and jet-lagged minds from our inward journeys, everyone agreed it was just what we all needed.

Now I know that the parkrun concept was slowly but surely spreading its wings to other countries worldwide, and I had reaped the benefits myself in Sydney and Brisbane less than eight months previously but, sadly, parkrun hadn't yet reached Argentina. When it does, as I'm sure it will, the wide paths, gentle gradients and stunning ocean view would make that nature reserve a perfect location for a Buenos Aires parkrun.

* * * * *

A few hours later, we gathered again in the lobby before venturing to the waterside bars and restaurants for an evening meal. After a couple of cold local beers, which went down so well after the hot run, we broke off into smaller groups to find the cuisine of our choice. Rupert, a guy called Ryan, a yachtsman from San Diego, and I opted for a beef restaurant and a special offer of a four-course meal, with each course being accompanied by a different glass of wine. The food was superb, as were the wines, but it was not to be my finest hour. Although the total amount of alcohol I consumed that evening did not seem to me particularly excessive, the effect it had on me was pretty dramatic, and I was certainly more worse for wear than I had been for many a year. Although I wasn't physically sick, I had no recollection of our actually settling the restaurant bill and had to check with Rupert the next morning that I had actually paid my share. I do remember some of the walk back to the hotel, and crossing the iconic Puente de la Mujer bridge, but largely because I was finding it so hard to walk in a straight line or even to keep upright. Indeed, judging by the photos taken by Ryan on his phone, it was only with the physical support of Rupert that I made it back safely. After only knowing each other since that very morning, the poor chap must have wondered how on earth he ended up sharing a room with this old guy who clearly couldn't hold his drink.

Curiously, the following morning, I had no sign of a hangover at all. At the very least, I deserved the dry mouth and banging headache that often ensues after a heavier-than-normal red wine session. In contrast, poor Rupert felt really ill the whole of the following morning and was himself physically sick – it didn't seem fair.

In retrospect, I look back upon that evening and wonder why I was so badly affected by what was not an unusually excessive amount of alcohol. The 14-hour flight, during which I had had a couple of glasses of wine, would have dehydrated me and a run, along with the sudden and dramatic rise in temperature, would only have exacerbated this. I won't pretend I don't enjoy a glass of beer or wine, but in moderation, and my usual weekly consumption is well within the so-called healthy guidelines. This was rather more than that but on a par with occasional family get-togethers, which leave me relatively unscathed. Nevertheless, it was a warning. I had a very tough half marathon coming up in a week's time and I vowed not to make that same mistake again before race day.

* * * * *

Day two in Buenos Aires began with a guided city tour on board a coach. If anything, the weather was even hotter and more humid than the day before. The central hub of Buenos Aires is the Plaza de Mayo, a potentially beautiful square with tall palm trees and picturesque gardens but which was currently hosting what appeared to be a construction site at its very centre.

Our coach circled the ornate presidential palace, Casa Rosada, which curiously is painted pink, apparently to distinguish it from the White House in Washington DC. We paused to visit the interior of the Catedral Metropolitana, which houses some important art relics, and marvelled at the spectacular column entrance of Argentina's National Bank. Our guide took us further afield to see the Floralis Generica, a giant steel and aluminium sculptured rose, standing 75 feet high, with the petals opening and closing with the sun. We then moved on to a rather more austere location: the La Recoleta Cemetery, the final resting place of many of Argentina's most rich and famous, including presidents and Nobel prize winners and perhaps most notably, Evita Perón.

Our journey took us on to the home of Buenos Aires' most famous football club, the blue and yellow-painted stadium of Boca Juniors, La Bombonera, where Diego Maradona plied his trade in his earlier years, before we then disembarked to discover, on foot, the Caminito, in the La Boca neighbourhood of the city, which is essentially a street art museum along an alleyway lined with brightly painted shanty homes and decorated with murals and sculptures.

It is impossible to get any real sense of a city from a single half-day excursion, but the variety of locations we had been introduced to highlighted both ends of the social divide, from the very affluent to the poor, and certainly demonstrated the country's rich artistic heritage, although barely scratching the surface of its complex political history.

* * * * *

The logistics of the Antarctica marathon, with a limit to the number of people being allowed to set foot on the continent in any one day, meant that the race had to take place over two days to accommodate the 200 or so runners. Two separate ships, our own, the *Ioffe*, and its sister ship, the *Vavilov*, would therefore be travelling out to Antarctica with a 24-hour gap between them, with the corresponding itinerary for the two cohorts being shifted by the same time gap. This did mean that we would be mixing with the *Vavilov* party on very few occasions, and this period in Buenos Aires was one of those. On this, our second day, the *Vavilov* passengers were arriving and the hotel suddenly became a whole lot busier.

Once again, a late-afternoon run in the ecological reserve was arranged, although this time it was much better attended, with both groups of runners taking part. I opted for the shorter route once more. While it was nice to stretch the legs and feel the inner glow that a run in unfamiliar surroundings brings, the heat was still very oppressive and

I was mindful of just how my body had reacted to those few drinks the night before.

I took a much more measured approach at our steak dinner that night with just a glass of local beer to accompany my meal. It was a chance to get to know a few more of our fellow passengers, including another Doug, a surgeon from Utah in the USA, who was also a veteran of the Marathon des Sables, just three years previously. At the end of the evening, our little group stood together on the 32nd floor of our hotel, looking down at the lights of the city below us. Between us, we had a vast amount of experience of running in all parts of the world and in all weather conditions, but there was a growing sense of awareness that we were on the verge of experiencing something really quite unique.

* * * * *

On our final full day in Buenos Aires, we were left to our own devices and Rupert and I wandered down to the famous San Telmo flea market, crammed full of traditional Argentinian handicrafts and antiquities laid out on cobbled streets and surrounded by colourful bohemian cafes and street musicians. The weather had thankfully turned considerably cooler, so much so that an afternoon attempt at working on a chapter of this book by the hotel rooftop pool was quickly curtailed by the strength of the wind blowing the printed pages around.

But now was the time to focus on the challenges ahead. With passengers from both ships now safely ensconced in the hotel, the evening was set aside for a cocktail reception, a welcome banquet and the all-important, and absolutely compulsory, pre-race briefing.

After picking up race T-shirts and the all-important luggage tags, which were essential for the efficient onward transport of our bags to the ship, the first task was to look at the cabin layout for *Ioffe*, and to see who my cabin-mate would be for the journey. Cabin 406 and Mike Morgan were the answers. We were all wearing handwritten name badges and it didn't take long to find Mike in the room. He was a tall, affable guy from Indianapolis, probably ten years my junior, who had recently retired from a large pharmaceutical company, so at least we had something in common straight away. Mike wasted no time in telling me that his biggest concern for my wellbeing on the journey was that he was a very loud snorer and he had even gone to the trouble of bringing earplugs with him for me to use. I politely declined for the time being but it was down to the humorous nature of our first meeting that I knew instantly that we would get on just fine on the trip.

After a meal of salmon, we listened intently as Jeff, the president of Marathon Tours, delivered the briefing. Nineteen different countries were represented and, for the first time in the race's 24-year history, there would be more women competitors than men, 99 as opposed to 94 males. At registration, 59 runners had entered the half marathon, the remainder running the full distance. However, full marathon runners had the option of converting to the half during the race if things weren't going particularly well, health or weather-wise, and would also be asked to stop at the half marathon distance if they hadn't reached that point before a cut-off time of three hours and ten minutes. Thankfully for me, there was no option of converting to the full distance once the race was under way! Interestingly, a record number of 31 competitors, including myself, stood to gain the coveted Seven Continents Club medal, either at the full or half marathon distance.

There was plenty of safety advice, too. The actual route to be run would be decided by the event crew the day before the race. In the past, it had been in a figure-of-eight shape to be run three times by the marathon runners and one and a half times by those running the shorter distance. However, in recent years, glacial melt brought on by climate change had made part of that route out towards a Uruguayan base unsafe, and we were warned to expect the same this year. For the first time, the event would be chip timed using devices on our wrists, but the most important advice was to get back on board the ship as quickly as possible after completing as, when the running stopped, our bodies would cool down very quickly in Antarctic conditions, and falls in air temperature of over 20°F in the space of ten minutes were not uncommon.

There were also some very serious ecological issues to consider as well. The Antarctica Environmental Protocol, which came into force in 1998, just 20 years previously, committed the signatories to the 'comprehensive protection of the Antarctic environment', and designated the continent as a 'natural reserve, devoted to peace and science'. We were extremely privileged to be allowed to set foot on this unique, non-political part of the planet, and it was no secret that certain international agencies were scrutinising the viability of allowing running events on King George Island. Time and time again, we were reminded that the only thing we could leave behind in Antarctica would be our footprints in the snow.

* * * * *

After barely a couple of hours of sleep, we were on board a bus taking us to the domestic airport in Buenos Aires, for our very early-morning flight south to Ushuaia. My relative mental calm with how the trip had unfolded so far had been disrupted by a message from home that my daughter, Angela, who was celebrating her birthday that very day, was unwell and needed to get an urgent appointment with her doctor. In itself, there was little I could do in the circumstances being so far away, but my concern was exacerbated by the fact that I knew that, once our ship left Ushuaia in just a few hours' time, we would have no internet or social media for the next ten days. Normally, that might be a cause for celebration but, in the circumstances, it was a major concern for me and, for the first time on the trip, I felt my anxiety building to worrying levels.

The flight to Ushuaia took just over three hours and there were stunning views over the lakes and snow-capped mountains of Patagonia as we began our descent. On the coach journey from the airport itself and into the city, our guide described some of the historical background of the city, which housed a large naval base. So remote was its location that people had to be given financial incentives to live there, and paid no income tax or VAT, and the stores paid less import duty compared to the rest of Argentina. Aside from a thriving fishing industry, the main work in the city was with the assembly of electrical goods from components shipped into the harbour. Wages were high and, with the tax advantages as well, people who settled in Ushuaia found it a hard place to move on from.

We had several hours to spend in Ushuaia before boarding our ship. It was a pleasant sunny day and some of the more energetic people in our party took a hike up to a glacier overlooking the city. With Rupert, Ryan and Renato, a Brazilian medic, I opted for the less strenuous option of investigating the steep and narrow streets of Ushuaia, which were lined with a strange mix of architecture from wooden houses with corrugated iron roofs intermingled with modern concrete buildings, prefabs and very basic wooden shanties.

After first visiting the tourist information office to have our passports stamped with a memento of our visit to the most southerly city on the planet, we climbed to the main shopping street, where shops competed for your custom with the reduced prices they could offer. Outside one shop, which had a large pig carcass rotating on a spit in the front window, several street dogs lay salivating on the pavement, in the hope that they might pick up some scraps.

Being a major naval base, the city had an expansive memorial site to the Argentinians lost during the Falklands War in 1982, which they, of course, called the War of the Malvinas. It was a little uncomfortable walking round there and reading the names of the many lost, for they had families as well, but I would have to say that both in Buenos Aires and here in this naval city, I encountered no overt signs of any anti-British sentiment.

We found a café that, apart from offering splendid coffee, gave us free wifi, allowing me to send out a few more messages back home to try and find out how Angela was. I was not great company that day, as my mind was elsewhere, but my colleagues, whom I had made aware of what was going on at home, were as supportive and understanding as ever.

Some of our group wanted to buy a bottle of spirits to take on the ship journey, so we perused the local supermarket shelves for the best whisky bargains. I do enjoy an occasional glass of whisky, but with my abject red wine experience in Buenos Aires still fresh in my mind, I passed on that one. And then it was time for lunch and our guide and others had told us that, when in Ushuaia, it is almost the law to sample the king crab. I opted for the slightly easier experience of a pasta dish with king crab and prawns, while others went for the full experience of dissecting a whole crab, suitably armed with a cutting tool to get inside the shell and claws. Verdict: tasty, very tasty.

Throughout the day, I had been sending messages back home and finally got a reassuring response from Angela herself, assuring me that she would be okay and not to worry and to just enjoy my adventure. Easier said than done, but I knew I could apply for a very basic email account on board the ship, so at least I wouldn't be entirely out of contact.

Soon, it was time for us all to meet up again to board the coach that would take us round to the ferry port. From our viewpoint, we could see our ship, MV *Ioffe*, at its moorings. It was completely dwarfed by a huge cruise liner behind it, moored on the other side of the harbour arm. For us, this would be no luxury cruise. As a bit of an aside, but perhaps a demonstration of how small our world can be, after I finally returned home a couple of weeks later, I discovered that a friend of mine from my home town of Redditch was actually on that liner on a cruise around the Argentinian and Chilean coasts of South America and that, unbeknown to each other, we had actually been in Ushuaia on that very same day.

When our coach pulled up alongside the ship, Liz, one of the superb staff of One Ocean Expeditions, who would manage the whole trip, boarded our coach and asked us all to surrender our passports for safe keeping. While some were reluctant to hand over such a vital document, Liz assured us that they would all be stored securely in a dry bag, so that if the ship did go down, at least our passports would be safe!

By late afternoon, I was on board and unpacking as best I could in my cabin. It was very cramped but the bunk felt comfortable and that was all that mattered. Offered the choice of bunks by Mike, I opted for the one next to the porthole window, although it took me a while to work out how to close it fully; Antarctica is not really the place you want to sleep next to a draughty window. It was time now to put on the first hyoscine patch just behind one ear and to dig out my acupuncture bracelets to go on my wrists. I wondered whether they were a genuine option or just a gimmick, but I was willing to give anything a try to hopefully prevent any recurrence of that childhood nightmare on the high seas.

Over the cabin intercom, we were called to a safety briefing in the dining room, one deck down, and on the way I was surprised to find we were already under way, sliding gently along the sheltered waters of the Beagle Channel. I had heard no engine sounds from our cabin and, in my efforts to find suitable storage for all my belongings where I knew I could find them again, I hadn't even noticed us leave the dockside.

David Sinclair was the leader of our expedition, a New Zealander, a lawyer, a family man and a relentless traveller on polar expeditions with an encyclopaedic knowledge of all things related to life at the polar extremities of our planet. David explained that as there would always be several Davids amongst his team or his clients, he would henceforth be known by his nickname of Sinckers, which was perhaps not the most appropriate name on board a ship about to enter the notorious Drake Passage. One by one, he introduced us to the other members of the One Ocean staff and you will get to know some of these over the ensuing pages. Men and women, covering a variety of ages, each with a title covering their main role but every one of them capable of multi-tasking over a huge range of activities: a truly incredible, multi-talented group of people. We were given a brief ship orientation reminder – port and starboard, bow and stern – and asked not to enter deck two, which was occupied by the Russian crew. We were advised to Drake-proof our cabins! This notorious expanse of ocean has a character that varies between the extremes of the placid Drake Lake to the tempestuous Drake Shake. Anything loose on a table top or cupboard would undoubtedly slide around or even fall on to the floor, which is not great when you are sleeping at night. Finally, we were sent back to our cabins to await the alarm signal for the compulsory lifeboat drill, which had to take place within the first couple of hours of departure. The instructions were simple. Wear as much warm clothing as possible and don the life vests that were to be found in the cabin. Quite simply, very few ships are to be found in that vast expanse of ocean and if we were to be unfortunate enough to take to the lifeboats, it could be days rather than hours before help could reach us.

Sadly, being from a port side cabin, we came second in the unofficial contest to see which side could evacuate and be ticked off on the register first. We hoped there wouldn't be a rematch.

* * * * *

We were soon enjoying our first experience of on-board cuisine at dinner. Four courses; soup, salad bar, main course and dessert and the quality was good. In the company of Larry, Cindy, Sheri, Mike and Rupert, I even risked a glass or two of red wine with my salmon main course. We were served at the table by the Russian ladies who doubled as cabin housemaids in the morning, many of whom were the partners of the male crew; a level of service that I hadn't expected.

It had been a long day since that very early call at the hotel in Buenos Aires for our flight on to Ushuaia, but there was time for a brief walk around the outer decks as the sun set lower in the sky. We slid past Puerto Williams in Chile; the southernmost town in the world as opposed to Ushuaia being the southernmost city. The waters in the Beagle Channel remained placid as we continued west and there was just time for a quick glass of beer in the ship's bar before bedtime; all part of finding our way round the ship, of course!

* * * * *

I woke briefly in the early hours. The orientation of my bunk ran along the length of the ship and I was being rocked gently from side to side in what was frankly quite a comforting fashion. We had left the calm waters of the Beagle Channel behind us; now we were heading south across the Drake Passage.

Chapter 13

Maxwell hitches a ride

'Good morning' – one or two seconds' pause – 'Good morning everybody.' And so began Sinckers' morning message that woke us from our slumbers the following day, and would indeed wake us for the next nine mornings as well. It became a signature part of the trip and, after we had all returned home and were sharing our memories via social media, Ryan revealed that he had recorded one of Sinckers' morning messages, and we all clambered for a copy just to relive it. No harsh sounds from a bedside alarm snapping you back to reality, just the calm dulcet tones of a voice gently bringing you to your senses and providing you with an update on what had happened while we had slept, and what we might expect from the day ahead.

Where were we now? How far across the Drake Passage had we travelled or, when we had finally reached Antarctica, were we still on the move or were we at anchor? He gave us wind speed and direction, the temperature of both the water and the air outside and the immediate weather forecast. Perhaps it had snowed while we slept, making the decks outside icy and slippery, and we could digest this information as we slowly came to. The morning message would always conclude with the time that fruit smoothies would be available in the bar, with the restaurant being open for breakfast 15 minutes later.

The ship would often be visited by birds as we headed south and Sinckers would update us on what had been spotted during the night. We had been asked not to leave lights on in the cabins as these were likely to attract birds who might then hitch a lift on board the ship. While the albatrosses and petrels could rest on the water's surface, even in quite stormy conditions, other birds needed a more solid resting place which, unbeknown to them, was taking them into uncharted territory.

One such bird was Maxwell, a cattle egret and a native of the South American continent. Named after the bay that we would be anchoring in for the race ahead, Maxwell had unwittingly hitched a lift on board a ship that was taking him to conditions he wouldn't be likely to survive in. Fortunately, the One Ocean staff had managed to contain him, and he was held captive and cared for on the ship, in the hope that he could be released once we returned towards Tierra del Fuego.

During one morning message, Sinckers solemnly announced that there had been a death on board the ship during the night. Had Maxwell succumbed to the deteriorating conditions? Fortunately, he hadn't and the death that morning was the bar's blender, meaning no more smoothies until it could be repaired.

✳ ✳ ✳ ✳ ✳

We had been allowed a good lie-in on that first morning as the previous day had been a very long one indeed. I was heartened by the fact that I didn't feel the slightest bit seasick, the only downside being that the acupuncture wrist bands were quite itchy, but I was prepared to put up with that. I managed to eat a good breakfast, the sea was relatively smooth and it was quite sunny outside. I also felt a great sense of relief when I set up my email account on the ship, sent a quick message home and got a response from both Angela and Chris. It was a very rudimentary system – no attachments or photographs – but at least I could keep in touch.

One of the appealing features of the journey was that the captain of the ship operated an open-bridge policy at certain times. As long as we remained quiet and kept towards the port side of the bridge, we could watch the crew at work and follow our progress on the many maps and charts available to us: an unusual insight into our unfolding adventure.

There was no chance of our getting bored on the two- to three-day journey on the way to Antarctica; there was a lot for us to learn from the safety point of view. First up was the fitting of our landing gear. There were no convenient jetties for *Ioffe* to tie up at, so shore landings, as well as the open water excursions, would be accomplished using the zodiacs, and for that we were called, deck by deck, down to what was known as the mudroom to be individually fitted with our bulky waterproof jackets, chest-high breeches and rubber gumboots. The jacket and breeches were to be kept in our cabins, making it even more cramped in there, but at least the boots, tagged with our cabin number, could live in the mudroom.

Now, depending on how great your thirst for knowledge was, there was every opportunity on board the voyage to keep right on top of whatever took your interest. If it was navigation, then a detailed log of the ship's position and heading was always available. If wildlife was your interest, posters around the ship described every species of bird or mammal we might encounter in this part of the planet. In addition, daily sightings of any species were also posted; the wandering albatross was indeed the most majestic sight as it followed the ship's course. The ship even had its own library, full of books on all aspects of our world's polar regions, from the incredible journeys of the early explorers to the geological transformations that had taken place over countless millions of years.

And then we had One Ocean's daily 'Ocean Notes' that were printed and displayed at strategic places on the stairways and corridors of the ship and which included a Russian word of the day to help us communicate with those working on the ship for us. Today's word was 'dobre outra' for 'good morning'. On this, our first full day at sea, we also learned from the 'Ocean Notes' about the geological history of the Drake Passage, which only opened up a mere 40 million years ago, and we were given tips on how to develop our sea legs and avoid the dreaded sickness that crossing the passage is so infamously associated with.

The 'Ocean Notes' would also contain the daily programme of events but Sinckers had made it very clear that this was only Plan A. Once we actually reached Antarctica, we were very much at the mercy of the weather and Plan A was very likely to transform into Plan B, C or even D at a moment's notice, such were the vagaries of the climate. At every single mealtime, breakfast, lunch and dinner, Sinckers would give an update on the latest information, as well as the occasional ticking-off, as happened on this first day when we were requested not to attempt to climb the ship's mast as somebody had done! I don't know if we ever found out who the culprit was.

There were two lectures that day down in the presentation room, which was on the deck below the Russian crew deck and had a reputation for being a bit bumpy when the Drake Passage was showing its teeth. Fortunately, it was still treating us kindly. The first was by Thom Gilligan, the founder of Marathon Tours way back in 1979, which was actually two years before I ran my very first mile. Thom was the man with the foresight to recognise that there was a market out there for people who wanted to run distance races in remote parts of the planet, and indeed to do this on all seven continents. At the time, the idea of organising a marathon in Antarctica seemed crazy to say the least, but Thom set about doing precisely that and had had to overcome a multitude of political barriers before creating the first event in 1994. It certainly hadn't been plain sailing, if that is an appropriate term to use in this context, since, and as I mentioned before, there were still agencies out there that believed this unique environment should not be hosting distance running events. Year by year,

Thom took us through each annual race, a few being described as relatively uneventful, but the majority incorporating some sort of drama, either with the athletes, the weather, the safety of the underfoot conditions or indeed the reliability of the partner ship operators who took responsibility for transporting the athletes out there.

In 1997, weather conditions were so bad that it proved impossible to get the competitors onshore and the marathon was held by running hundreds of laps around the decks of the ship and then, of course, in 2016, the year I so nearly picked up a last-minute place, blizzards and deteriorating sea conditions led to the captain of the ship ordering the evacuation of all on land before some of them, including my Kiwi friend, Jan, had completed their marathon distance. Sadly, the ships currently used for the expeditions were not suitable for laps of the deck, so a few were unable to complete the full distance.

It was a fascinating insight into the background of this race and a further reminder of just how unique it was. Secretly, we all hoped that when Thom repeated his presentation before the 2019 race, the 2018 event would rank in his 'relatively uneventful' category.

The second lecture that day related to something that had been playing on my mind for a number of months, ever since I had started perusing the photographs of previous events: the opportunity to go sea kayaking in the icy waters of Antarctica. The pictures looked amazing but would it be safe for me as a non-swimmer? If people wanted to sign up for kayaking on the trip, and it was reasonably expensive, then the kayak meeting was mandatory. I decided to go along and make a decision after I had all the information.

Liz and Natalie from One Ocean were the kayak instructors and delivered a thorough demonstration of how the sessions would be organised, the selection process as the number of kayaks was limited on any one excursion, the wetsuit, life jacket and safety procedures and, of course, the fact that all of the sessions were highly dependent on there being safe sea conditions. There were single and double kayaks available. I certainly wouldn't have risked the single but maybe I could have paired up with somebody who was experienced, but then that would have put an unfair burden on them as, if we were to have capsized, it was a pretty fair bet I would have been a very panicky individual for them, and the instructors, to deal with. In the end, common sense got the better of my curiosity and I left the kayak meeting without signing the disclaimer form that I would have needed. At least I would still experience being close to the water in the zodiacs.

* * * * *

When we woke the following morning, we were officially in Antarctica. From the outer decks of the ship, only ocean was visible; no sign of land or ice yet, but we had crossed the invisible 60 degrees south latitude line that demarcates Antarctica, a point beyond which even Donald Trump's Twitter account cannot reach – or at least that was what Sinckers told us!

Once again, sea conditions had been kind to us overnight; the gentle side-to-side rocking of my bunk helping me towards a really comfortable night's sleep. It would be another full day on the open seas but there was a very busy programme planned to prepare us for what lay ahead. Immediately after breakfast, we attended a compulsory presentation about the role of the International Association of Antarctica Tour Operators, which promotes the practice of safe and environmentally responsible travel to this unique continent. We were left in no doubt of our responsibilities, not only as a group, but also as individuals. Nothing, absolutely nothing, that was not native to Antarctica should be introduced, so we would all be required to decontaminate everything we brought ashore, as well as stepping through trays of biocide, both before we left the ship and when we returned to it, to prevent microbial transfer.

This was followed by yet another mandatory briefing, this time on the safe use of the zodiac craft that we would be using for water excursions and shore landings. These were lowered from the ship's stern by crane and individually piloted by the vast majority of the One Ocean crew, whatever their other responsibilities were. To access the zodiacs, we were first checked to see that our life vests had been suitably tightened, as these would be what was grabbed if you were unfortunate enough to end up in the water, and you wouldn't want to slip out! Then we climbed down a steep, and sometimes slippery, stepped gangway down the side of the ship to a platform at water level, where a member of the Russian crew was waiting to help us get on and off. This was quite easy when the waters were calm but less so when the wind was blowing and the zodiac was moving up and down quite some considerable distance relative to the gangway platform.

The following few hours were spent decontaminating everything I planned to take ashore for the race, which was now just two days away. My trail shoes, which I planned to run in, have encountered a variety of surfaces in their time and after a particularly muddy run will get a good scrub and hosing down to return them to a wearable condition. Now I was expected to return them to pristine condition and with the deep grooves you get in the soles of trail shoes to give you better grip, those last few specks of dried mud can be hard to dig out. Armed with scrubbing brushes and a penknife blade, and sat beside a tray of the biocidal fluid on deck, I toiled away. A couple of times I offered what I thought was a pretty clean pair of shoes for inspection by Harry of One Ocean, only to receive a shake of the head and have a few more fragments pointed out. Eventually, I got the nod; my shoes at least were worthy of a shore visit!

This then left my running suit, rucksack, bumbag and Camelbak to clean up, although at least I could do this in the relative warmth of the ship's interior. Equipped with one of several vacuum cleaners placed around the ship, I set out to remove every blade of grass, seed, cat hair or any other debris, not the easiest of tasks when there was Velcro to contend with as well. Eventually my job was done; my equipment was race ready.

There were two more lectures to attend that afternoon; Liz gave us some very valuable tips on photography in the Antarctic and Sinckers gave us an insight into the wildlife we might expect to see, some of which was potentially feisty. We were then issued with our race numbers and timing wrist bands; number 199 for me – the race of a lifetime was edging closer.

By the time we woke the next morning, we would be anchored in Maxwell Bay off the shore of King George Island and we all squeezed into the presentation room to hear what Sinckers had in store for us, or at least what Plan A was, as he once again reinforced. The Marathon Tours team would be going ashore to recce and mark out the race course. For some of those who had signed up, there would be an opportunity for a kayak outing, weather permitting, of course. The rest of us would be taking our first zodiac cruise out to Ardley Island in Maxwell Bay, half of us before lunch, half of us after. Excitement was building.

※ ※ ※ ※ ※

The Drake Passage had a little sting in its tail. Throughout the night, I had felt aware that the gentle side-to-side rocking motion was being mixed with more vigorous head-to-toe pitching, and a couple of times I grabbed at the table top next to the bunk to stop myself from falling out. At around 4am, I was woken by a loud bang and the whole ship shuddered. Had we hit an iceberg? I lay there half expecting to hear the alarm call for us to don life jackets but, apparently, it was just a large wave. Unbeknown to me, my cabin mate, Mike, had crept out after the loud bang to go to the library, from which he had seen amazing views of driving snow and waves breaking over the bow of the ship.

As I struggled to get back to sleep, and despite having been completely silent for three days, my mobile phone suddenly chirped into life with a text message. It was just after 5am and I stretched my hand out from under the blanket in the darkness to reach for it. It was a message from my network operator saying 'Welcome to Chile' and giving details of the reduced roaming charges that were available to me. This was not something that needed my immediate attention, so I placed the phone back on the bedside table, rolled over and tried again to sleep. Exactly 52 minutes later, the phone sounded again and, once more, I was woken. For goodness sake! This time the screen welcomed me to China and offered similar roaming charges, but this time I couldn't get back to sleep so quickly. Chile to China in less than an hour? The two countries are on opposite sides of the planet; subsequent research showed they are separated by over 12,000 miles. Short of hitching a lift on the International Space Station, that was plainly impossible.

There is only one part of our planet where this scenario could possibly happen. Our ship was fast approaching the South Shetland Islands in politically-neutral Antarctica and my phone was picking up network signals from the international research bases on King George Island. We had well and truly arrived in Antarctica.

I drew the curtains back from our cabin window and got my first view of King George Island; rocky, snowy and ice-covered in places but certainly not totally white. After breakfast, I ventured out on to the slippery decks to take some photographs. Snow was still falling and it was bitterly cold, so my hands were out of my gloves just long enough to press the shutter button. In the water, penguins were swimming by and we got our first distant view of a whale, although too far away to identify.

Looking towards King George Island, we could see the prefabricated buildings of the Russian Bellingshausen station from where our race would start. Above it, on a hillside, stood the Russian Orthodox, wooden Trinity church, shipped in parts by the *Ioffe*'s sister vessel, the *Vavilov*, and reassembled by the station's staff. To the west, the red sheds and storage tanks of the Chilean base could be seen.

With our zodiac cruise scheduled for the afternoon, I spent most of the morning checking and re-checking my kit for race day. Foil sachets of gel were emptied into my new gel flask and the insulated Camelbak was half-filled with water. Most runners were intending to leave numbered bottles at designated points on the route but, as I have said many times before, I prefer the sip-sip approach, even in these icy conditions. The memories of my half marathon in Siberia, when I became so dehydrated, were still very vivid even many years later.

It was no easy matter to keep track of time, either. Both my watch and my phone were repeatedly picking up signals from the Russian, Chilean and Chinese bases on the island and displaying their own local times, and not both at the same time either, so there were occasions when there was a ten-hour difference between my watch and phone, and yet neither was right! Technology, eh! In the end, I would regularly check the analogue clock at the ship's reception desk as a reference.

* * * * *

After lunch, it was time for our first zodiac cruise and Mike and I put on plenty of layers before donning our wet suits in the cabin and waiting to be called down to the mudroom to put on our boots and life vests. It was still very cold and I wore two layers of gloves; a thin, inner pair that I could keep on to take photographs and the windproof and waterproof outer pair that I would be using for the race itself.

We queued at the head of the gangway before we were checked in, had our life vests tightened and then, one by one, descended the steps to the platform at water level. Harry was our pilot for this first trip. Between him in the craft and the Russian sailor on the platform, we were guided safely on board using the hand-to-elbow grips we had been taught and successive steps on to the rim, a wooden stool and then the floor of the craft, before sitting on the edge and sliding down to our final position.

The zodiacs took between ten and 12 passengers and, once we were full, we drifted away from the side of the ship, where we paused while Harry explained the 'man overboard' procedures. As he said, the most likely person to fall off would be him, as he would be standing in order to operate the outboard motor, but he did have a 'dead man's handle' around his wrist, which would cut the engine in the event of him and the zodiac parting company.

With that, we sped away towards Ardley Island at a rate that I initially found a little disconcerting, and I was glad of the rope around the perimeter of the craft that I could hang on to. We soon had a very quick introduction to life, and indeed death, in the Antarctic environment. An unlucky penguin, porpoising through the waters, had been taken between the jaws of a leopard seal, and was being shaken violently from side to side to strip it of its feathers and skin. From the skies, seabirds descended in numbers to pick up any scraps from the now blood-stained water's surface.

There were more pleasant scenes to view as well. Rocky shorelines alive with penguin activity, of both the Gentoo and Chinstrap species, and we watched, captivated by their activities. Who doesn't love a penguin? Close by, another large leopard seal wobbled awkwardly across the stony ground on the shore before silently slipping into the icy water, where it was immediately transformed into a skilful predator. And there were floating icebergs; fairly small ones at this location but far more mass lurked beneath the surface. A penguin was trying to negotiate a steepish downward slope on one of the small bergs when it lost its footing and comically fell flat on its back. Just as a cat does when it misjudges a jump, it sprang back upright and immediately looked around as if to say 'I hope nobody noticed that'.

Harry took us closer into the shoreline of King George Island, where we could get a better view of the Russian, Chilean and Chinese bases. And then we were treated to a rare sight as a huge Hercules aircraft descended noisily overhead to land on the island's airstrip and to bring in supplies to those for whom this was home, albeit temporarily.

Up until this point, I had been relatively comfortable out on the water. My head and ears were well protected by a woolly hat and my body kept warm by multiple thermal layers. Even with two pairs of gloves, the ends of my fingers, and particularly both thumbs, were really beginning to feel quite cold and painful, probably because I was constantly taking the outer gloves on and off to take photos of our spectacular surroundings. I rubbed my hands vigorously together and tried to warm my fingertips under my armpits.

As if to demonstrate to us just what it was capable of, the Antarctic suddenly produced a lively squall out of nowhere. The wind whipped up the surface of the water and, as Harry headed us back towards the safety of the ship, the waves were getting larger by the minute and we were being tossed around and peppered by spray and stinging ice pellets. It was an uncomfortable return journey but even more so for those who had been selected for their sea kayaking experience that afternoon. In conditions in which the expedition would not have been permitted to start, the recovery of those kayakers tested the skills of all those involved.

* * * * *

At dinner that evening, we listened intently as Thom gave us the final race briefing. As expected, and in line with what had happened over recent years, the route out towards the Uruguayan base was too hazardous, so we would be running the loop from Bellingshausen out to the Chinese Great Wall base and back again; six loops for the full marathon and three for the half. This did mean that we would be seeing quite a lot of one another during the race as we passed running to and fro, which was reassuring after experiencing just how quickly the weather could change. Thom reminded us that one of the conditions that allowed the race to go ahead was that we made no use of any of the indoor facilities at any of the bases so, although we would be coming ashore in our zodiac gear, we would have to store this in our now super-clean bags and prepare for the race on some tarpaulins, weighted down by rocks, on the shoreline. Using the Antarctic as a toilet was also strictly forbidden, so a single tented cubicle would be erected in the start/finish area containing little more than a barrel.

A lot of water was being drunk at dinner that evening, in contrast to the nights before and after, and the vast majority of us headed straight to bed afterwards in readiness for a 6am Sinckers alarm call. Race day had almost arrived.

* * * * *

I was on board one of the very first zodiacs ashore the next morning after a light breakfast of watermelon, a pastry and some coffee. My choice of what to wear for the run had been pretty straightforward – the fleece-lined, windproof and waterproof running suit had served me well in Siberia and on Greenland's ice cap, and it would do the same here. On top of that I wore the red and yellow vest of the Midlands Air Ambulance charity that I was fundraising for: we had been advised to wear some bright colours to stand out in any photographs. The running suit had a hood but I also wore a woolly hat that would fit more tightly over my ears, always a vulnerable point in sub-zero conditions. I opted for just the one pair of gloves, again with protection against both wind and water, as I knew my hands would soon warm up once the running started, and my hands are usually the first part of me that tends to get overheated. I threw a lighter pair of gloves into my bag as well just in case the weather turned for the worse, along with my goggles, trail shoes and bumbag containing my gel flask and small camera.

Of course, on top of all this, I had to put on my wet gear, the gumboots and the life-vest for the zodiac ride to the shore, so it was a pretty bulked-up version of me that clambered down the gangway, clutching my immaculately clean rucksack.

The icy water in Maxwell Bay was fairly calm that morning, so the ride to our landing spot was a lot smoother than the final few minutes of the zodiac cruise of the day before. Once we had reached the shallows, my bag was taken from me by the race crew, who were already ashore, and I swung my legs over the side of the zodiac, dropped into the icy water and waded to the shoreline. Finally, I was standing on the continent of Antarctica.

After adding my life vest to a growing pile on the rocky beach, I was directed to the tarpaulin that had been designated for the half marathon runners. As an early arrival, I had plenty of space to easily remove my jacket and breeches, although getting back out of the boots proved to be far more problematic as my fingertips were already feeling very cold. I slid the boots one inside the other to ensure they remained as a pair for my return journey. Having squashed my wet gear into my rucksack, and put on my goggles, trail shoes and bumbag, I wandered around the Russian base trying to find a variety of different surfaces and to make sure I had sufficient grip from my shoes. The advice that we wouldn't need to wear spikes or studded soles seemed to be pretty sound.

As runner-filled zodiacs continued to arrive in larger numbers, the tarpaulins became more and more congested as people struggled to find space to change. Then, out of nowhere, the Antarctic decided to show its power and threw a blizzard at us. The skies above suddenly took on a yellowish tinge and snow started to tumble from them. With the start time fast approaching, I asked a running friend to take a photo of me standing beneath the start/finish banner. He must have been shivering like crazy as the resulting image was just a big blur, but I didn't have the heart to ask him to do it again. We bounced up and down trying to keep warm. I wear varifocal lenses when I'm running as I need good near vision to avoid any tripping hazards and longer vision to see what lies ahead. Over the top of these, I was wearing ski goggles and constantly needed to brush accumulated snowflakes off these.

Even though it had only been snowing for around 20 minutes, it was already piling up on the route. We were called to the start line. I placed myself near the back of the pack; there were some serious-looking athletes around me. A few final words of encouragement from Thom, a countdown and we were away. I was running in Antarctica!

* * * * *

I set off at a steady pace as we headed inland away from the shoreline cabins of the Russian base, initially downhill but very soon climbing up towards the Chilean base and the lights of the landing strip, which we had seen the Hercules aircraft heading towards the previous day. The snow was heavy but it brought benefits as well. Anyone who has run in freshly fallen snow knows that it gives good grip underfoot so the prospects of slipping and sliding about on ice were diminishing by the minute. The route was rocky and uneven and I was constantly turning my ankles over on stones hidden by the snow, so caution got the better of me. The last thing I needed was a badly twisted ankle; this was going to be a run to finish rather than aiming for a time. The route took a turn around the silent buildings of the Chilean base and then headed south but with a roller coaster trail of steep climbs and descents, which were already taking a toll on me. The snow was still falling heavily but I was warming to the run now and the numbness I had felt in my fingertips at the start was ebbing away. This was fun. This was a real adventure. Finally, we began a long descent and entered a fairly flat section with a large, partially frozen lake on our right-hand side. We passed the amazing Molly, one of the non-running partners on the trip who had volunteered to help during the race. Molly stood at the point where some of the runners had dropped off their labelled water bottles to grab a drink on each lap as they ran past. Molly was out there for nearly seven hours, not keeping warm by running as we were, but by dancing and singing constantly and yelling encouragement as runners went past in both directions; a performance that deserved a medal in its own right. Even as I reached that first lake, the lead runners were already running back towards me on their first return journey. Some were easily recognisable and we exchanged a few words of mutual encouragement. Some were so heavily swathed in their protective clothing I had no idea who they were, but we still exchanged a word, a wave or a high five anyway.

I'd already taken advantage of trying out my fuelling strategy and was happy I'd made the right decisions. The insulation on the Camelbak meant there was no chance of water freezing in the narrow drink tube and, why had I not discovered the flexible gel flask before? Although many people don't get on with them, I always use gels in any race of ten miles or over, but it can be a tricky business tearing off the end of the foil wrapper whilst running and then having to consume the whole lot. Almost inevitably you end up with gel on your hands, leaving your fingers uncomfortably sticky for the rest of the run. Not only did the flask let you take the gel a little at a time, but the bite valve kept your hands clean. Definitely a lesson learned for future distance races.

Our husband and wife race medical team of Ellen, the doctor, and Peter, the paramedic, drove up and down the course on a motorised buggy to keep an eye on all of us as the snow continued to fall. The instructions were simple. They would give you a thumbs-up as they drove past. If you were good, you gave a thumbs-up in return. If you were struggling, you gave a thumbs-down and they would stop and help. Shortly after the lake we reached the shoreline and now the route was much flatter, although littered with a mix of slush and mud, which penetrated my trail shoes and chilled my toes. Penguins watched us from the rocky beach and occasionally waddled across our path, happily ignoring the yellow 'penguin crossing' signs that had been placed there for their benefit by the race crew.

A turn to the left and more rocky trail led us to the turnaround point outside the Chinese Great Wall base, manned nobly by Larry. We were to hear later of Larry's heroic actions in chasing a leopard seal off the route during the course of the race. Our volunteers were awesome.

It continued to snow for much of the return journey on that first leg, but becoming less and less heavy, and by the time I got back to the Russian base the sun was beginning to creep through the cloud which, in Antarctica, usually meant that the temperature began to drop as the skies cleared.

A call of nature meant I spent a little longer at the base than I had hoped as I joined a short queue to use the race toilet facility. Remember, turning the snow yellow in Antarctica was definitely not permitted.

Off I went on my second lap and this time the uphill climbs in particular were becoming increasingly arduous; I had my hands clamped to the front of my thighs as I drove my way up them. The downhill sections gave some respite but, on the second return journey, the consequences of the drop in temperature were becoming apparent as the route became more and more slippery, with the pounding feet of the runners compressing the snow that had given us such a good grip previously. Maybe the studded soles that were back in my cabin might have been useful after all.

By the time I got back to the Russian base at the end of my second loop, my pace had dropped considerably. I was walking most of the steep uphill sections and now being cautious on the downhills as well because of the ice. Up until now I had not used the small camera I carried in my bumbag, as pulling it out and taking the heavy gloves on and off to take photographs would only have wasted more time. My hands were now quite warm from the running, so I decided I would use my third and final loop to record some of the sights along the way. This meant another delay at the turnaround point as I tried to find my bag to change into a lighter pair of gloves that I wouldn't have to remove to take a picture.

I knew exactly where I had left my bag but it wasn't there – it had been moved. To compound the problem, all the bags now had a heavy layer of snow on them, so it took me quite some time to locate it. And then I was off again, but this time stopping occasionally to capture a scenic view. I thanked Molly for her encouragement and entertainment and I thanked Larry at the China base turnaround, pausing there while he took a photograph of me on a rocky incline. The weather hadn't finished with us yet, oh no. On the final return leg, the wind started to blow much harder into my face and even the buff pulled up over my nose and mouth provided little protection against the biting cold. On a downhill section in the final mile, I suddenly went into an uncontrollable ice-slide, waving my arms around frantically, but successfully, in an attempt to avoid an ungainly fall. A patch of fresh, untrodden snow brought me to a halt and saved my day.

And now small buildings came into sight. We were approaching the Bellingshausen base again for the third and final time. The realisation dawned on me that I was minutes away from fulfilling a lifetime's ambition and I wanted to make a mad dash for the finishing line, shouting to the world that I had done it! Common sense took over. I was still running on what was largely an ice rink, with no stabilising studs on my shoes, and a fall, and heaven forbid, a broken bone, would have been a rather ignominious ending to what had been such a long personal journey.

Running at the outer edges of the trail, where the snow was relatively untrodden, I rounded the final turn and saw the finish banner ahead of me. I was beaming from ear to ear, although that might not have been obvious with all the paraphernalia protecting my face and head from the elements. With arms outstretched, I crossed the finish line. I had completed at least a half marathon on every one of the planet's seven continents. Job done!

Chapter 14

A whale of a time

Having exchanged my wrist timing chip for an impressively heavy, penguin-themed finisher's medal, I made my way over to the tarpaulins to ready myself for the return zodiac trip back to the ship. We had been warned that we would cool down very rapidly in the Antarctic environment once we had finished running, and to get back to the ship as quickly as possible. They were not wrong, but it was easier said than done.

There was a zodiac with a few runners on it being held in the shallows and the pilot indicated that they would wait for me. I found my bag quickly enough, as it was still in the same place I had left it when I changed gloves before the last leg, but it had been separated from my boots. Dozens of pairs of identical boots to search through, many still covered in snow, looking for that tiny tag with my cabin number on. Found them! I had to take my trail shoes off to haul my waterproof breeches back on, while fumbling with the double-tied laces. Cold fingers, cold toes. I pulled the big, bulky jacket back on and zipped it up, and then dropped down on to the ground to try and haul those big, heavy boots back on. The zodiac pilot was trying to hurry me but if your fingers are numb with cold, it's not easy. A kind helper was already dropping a life vest over my head and tightening up the straps. I staggered into the icy water, sat on the rubberised edge of the boat, swung my legs inside and, in an instant, the outboard motor was racing us back to the *Ioffe*. Ten minutes later, I was standing beneath one of the most welcome hot showers I have ever had.

* * * * *

It didn't take too long to recover, although my body was strangely covered in bright orange patches and my hands remained very swollen for several hours. A lunchtime meal of chilli con carne and pear crumble was devoured in no time and a quick email home to tell everyone of my triumph got a rapid response from Chris, who told me that my story was featured on the BBC news website and that two BBC local radio stations wanted to interview me when I got home.

As time passed by, more and more runners returned from their race, mostly in joy, but there were a few disappointments as well: tales of withdrawal through sheer fatigue, several full marathon runners deciding to call it a day at the half marathon distance, and one of the faster marathon runners pulling a hamstring on his very first loop, but bravely hobbling on to complete the half distance.

By late afternoon, everybody was back on board and there was an air of wild celebration everywhere. Thom, and the other members of the Marathon Tours team, left the *Ioffe* and transferred across to the *Vavilov*, which was now anchored in Maxwell Bay. We lined the side of the ship to wave them off as they prepared to repeat the whole race experience for the *Vavilov* passengers the following day.

Now it was party time. A couple of glasses of Beagle Red beer before dinner, some red wine with the meal, and then back to the bar for a night of dancing, celebration and perhaps a few more drinks. Nate, from New Zealand, even managed to throw in an impromptu haka. There couldn't have been a happier bunch of people on the planet that night. Sadly, my party stamina is not what it was in my youth so, as tiredness began to overcome me, I stepped outside on to the deck to get a breath of fresh air before heading back to the cabin for some well-earned sleep. It was snowing heavily again, the ship was on the move, the driven snowflakes illuminated by the powerful navigation light beams from the ship. I could not have felt happier. What a day!

And back inside, the revelry went on well into the early hours of the next morning and I wouldn't have been surprised if some didn't get any sleep at all.

* * * * *

We were still sailing when we were woken the next morning as we approached Mikkelsen Bay for another shore landing. Sea conditions were pretty rough so the morning's kayaking excursion had to be cancelled. It turned out to be a fairly short visit as the weather deteriorated further, but it was certainly not without incident, heartbreak or beauty. The snow was deep as we came ashore and hundreds of penguins peered suspiciously at us as they waddled about their way. Two leopard seals on the shoreline were fighting a battle of supremacy, roaring and lunging at each other. We kept our distance. Out on the water, yet another penguin was meeting its end in the jaws of a leopard seal.

We came across a relic from the past in the form of the skeletal remains of an old wooden rowing boat from the days when whaling was permitted in the Antarctic, and then, as we returned to the ship, with the sea conditions being at the very limit of safety, two of our zodiacs were actually attacked by leopard seals, their teeth sinking into the rubberised exterior walls of the craft. Scary but not too dangerous as the rim of the boat was compartmentalised, so there was no danger of the whole craft deflating. Nevertheless, the pilots opened the throttle of the outboard motors and beat a hasty retreat, and the two damaged zodiacs were out of action for a day or two while repairs were carried out.

At lunch, our ship's doctor, Jackie, brought us the news that there was a cough virus going around the ship, and we were to be extra vigilant with our on-board hygiene procedures, including coughing into our elbows rather than on to our hands. So far, I had avoided it.

While we were eating, our ship had moved on into the nearby Cierva Cove and the purpose of the afternoon zodiac cruise was to hopefully spot some whales in this sheltered inlet.

What happened that day will remain with me for the rest of my life. As readers of *Running Hot & Cold* know, I have already experienced a very close encounter with a group of large mammals on a running trip, when our group of athletes, out walking in the bush, were chased by angry elephants in South Africa in 2012. That was scary, very scary; this could not have been more different.

No more than a minute or two after our mini-flotilla of three zodiacs left the gangway platform of *Ioffe*, in the search for whales, two magnificent humpback whales came and introduced themselves to us. The 15 minutes that followed I can only describe as magical and, even months later as I write this, it brings a lump to my throat and tears to my eyes. They were probably 35 to 40 feet long, at least twice as long as our vulnerable craft, and yet they could not have been more gentle. They swam alongside us, close enough for us to touch them if we had wanted to, but we didn't want to disturb the show they were putting on. They rolled on to their sides and their backs, their huge pectoral fins breaking the surface and slapping back down again. They blew spray from their blowholes as they circled in formation and, from time to time, their huge, knobbly heads would breach the surface just feet away from us, as if they were asking what we were doing there. They produced a variety of sounds, from deep guttural groans, clicking sounds and no doubt several more beyond my range of hearing. We were completely transfixed by the performance they were putting on for us. Even our experienced pilots, who had probably led these excursions several times before, had never seen anything quite like it. We were all in awe. Some described it as a religious experience and I could not dispute that. It certainly brought home to me, in that 15-minute encounter, that we share our world with some magnificent creatures and rarely take into account the effects of our actions and behaviour on them. I cannot describe how privileged I felt to have shared that time with those two whales but I would like my children, grandchildren and future generations to have the same opportunity. For that to happen, we all have to change our habits and I know those two humpbacks have now changed me.

As I climbed into my bunk at the end of that day, I wrote one final sentence into my diary: 'This is like a dream.'

* * * * *

By morning, we had moved on to Wilhelmina Bay, the sun was shining brightly and the scenery was staggering. Once again, the bay was alive with whales; our 'Ocean Notes' informed us that it is normally called Whalehelmina! We didn't have the close-up encounter that we had experienced the previous day but we were treated to elaborate displays of fluking as the humpbacks breached the surface and then went into a dive, throwing their unique tail flukes up above the surface to the sound of dozens of camera shutters. Just beautiful. Our zodiac pilot that morning was Kaylan from One Ocean, who had trained as an actress but had an encyclopaedic knowledge of everything Antarctican, and comfortably dealt with the myriad of questions we were throwing at her.

While our wildlife encounters had made such an impact on me, the scenery in Antarctica is like nowhere else on earth, and the bright sunshine and clear skies we enjoyed that morning truly enhanced the spectacular colours and shapes of the ice formations. Until that trip, I had not even been aware of blue ice but now it was all around us. Formed when air bubbles are squeezed out by the intense pressures within the glacial ice over tens, if not hundreds of thousands of years, the intensity of the colour could vary between a pale blue hue at the water level in icebergs that had recently calved off the edge of glaciers, to deep royal blue stripes in the glacial walls themselves. Whatever direction you pointed your camera, you could not fail to take an amazing photograph. And it wasn't just the colour of the ice either but the weird and wonderful sculpted shapes, varying from mushroom-shaped icebergs to one that truly resembled a giant bearded wizard, in a pointed hat, sitting on the edge of his own personal island.

* * * * *

Plan A for that afternoon had been that the passengers from the *Vavilov*, who had completed their race the previous day, would join us on the *Ioffe* for a joint celebration barbecue, but they were running a little behind their scheduled arrival, so Sinckers brought forward another of the highlights of the trip: the polar plunge.

Now, just over half of our passengers were game for this but I, as a non-swimmer, was not one of them. Nevertheless, it provided a great afternoon's entertainment as I watched from the ship's deck. The participants, or maybe that should be victims, queued patiently inside the ship in their swimwear, keeping warm in their white bathrobes. One by one, they were led out to the head of the gangway, disrobed themselves and had a safety harness fitted to them before being led gingerly down the gangway, pausing at the bottom to maybe say a few words into their personal video cams, and then plunging themselves into the icy Antarctic waters from the platform, before being hauled back out again. Brave souls. Some threw themselves in with complete abandon, others dipped a tentative big toe in first, and perhaps the most memorable polar plunger was the ebullient Jenney, a young lady from Boston who, having uttered her self-motivating words into her camera, paused for a short while on the platform as people on the deck noticed some surface disturbances on the water some 50 metres away. Jenney went for it anyway and on hitting the water was treated to a herd of fur seals rushing towards her.

They were harmless and veered off at the last moment. Luckily, they weren't leopard seals!

Eventually, the *Vavilov* did arrive and dropped anchor in the bay, a quarter of a mile away. Their passengers came across in their zodiacs and, for the first time, we had the opportunity to find out how their race had unfolded. The results from the two days, for both the half and full marathons, had been merged and posted and I was happy to see that, in the half marathon, I had placed 35th out of 82 competitors. My time of a few seconds over three hours had slightly disappointed me, but this was the Antarctic and time was irrelevant. The experience had been like nothing I had done before.

Now it was barbecue time! Yes, an outdoor barbecue on the stern deck of a former Russian research vessel in the coldest and most remote continent on the planet. We had to dress warmly but that didn't stop it from being one of the greatest parties ever. As music rang out across the frozen waters, meats and fish sizzled on the grills, and the range of vegetables, salads and breads was astounding, as were the desserts. And if that wasn't enough, the all-inclusive beer and wine flowed freely.

After we had filled our stomachs to capacity, Thom climbed on to a platform on the mast and announced the overall race winners, as well as those who had won their age categories in the marathon. Then came one of the proudest moments of my life. Thirty-one of us on that deck had completed their seven continents quest in the Antarctic and, after our names were read out, we were each presented with our Seven Continents Club medal by Jeff, the president of Marathon Tours, and so became part of an exclusive club that numbers only a few hundred people to date. It had been almost 37 years since that first one-mile run that I had found so unbelievably difficult, but now, as I approached the end of my seventh decade, I had run at least a half marathon on each of our world's seven continents and confronted many personal health issues, notably with mental wellbeing and self-belief, along the way. I am not one to blow my own trumpet, but I was pretty pleased with myself.

As before, the celebrations continued long after the *Vavilov* passengers had returned to their ship; wine flowed at dinner and the high jinks continued in the bar afterwards with Tessa, the barmaid, wearing a penguin costume and Andy, an outgoing Liverpool lad, and unquestionably the focal point of all hilarity, wearing the Superwoman costume that Laura, another British girl, had worn for the race. It is my experience that there is normally a celebration party after all of my epic foreign running adventures. This was different. Essentially, we were all trapped on a ship together with another full day to spend in Antarctica followed by another two and a half days of sailing back across the Drake Passage without the possibility of more running to distract us. This party had nowhere near run its course yet!

We formed a self-proclaimed *Ioffe* Badassery Club and enrolled each and every one of us. Badassery was not a word I was particularly familiar with, but apparently related to people who engage in apparently impossible activities, succeed against all the odds, thus stunning their disbelieving friends and family. It seemed pretty appropriate.

* * * * *

As we woke on our final morning in Antarctica, we were at anchor in the spectacular Paradise Harbour. After breakfast, we donned our wet gear for the very last time in the mudroom before setting off in the zodiacs for a shore landing at a deserted Argentinian base, which was closed for the winter. After scrambling over the rocky shoreline, the snow on the slopes was really quite deep. We were now standing on the Antarctica peninsula itself and had the opportunity to climb a steep hill to a vantage point with spectacular views of the surrounding snow- and ice-covered mountains. I made it about halfway up, my gumboots providing little grip as I slipped and slithered my way onwards but, disappointingly, I called it a day there as the ship cough virus was beginning to trouble me and I climbed back down to spend the rest of our limited time onshore exploring the Argentinian Brown Station, named after Admiral William Brown, the father of the Argentine navy. On the snowy slopes, and all around the deserted wooden buildings, Gentoo penguins were everywhere.

Now, another of the rules we were asked to abide by when in Antarctica was that we did not approach closer than five metres to any wildlife. Clearly, the penguins did not have the same rules. As I sat on my own in the snow, curious penguins would tentatively toddle towards me, making photographic opportunities oh so simple. They truly are delightful and inquisitive creatures. Even a snowy sheathbill, the only land bird native to Antarctica, and therefore not having webbed feet, came within inches of my rubber boots, eyeing me with a mixture of suspicion and curiosity. Much further away, two leopard seals were arguing noisily at the water's edge, but then you wouldn't want to get closer than five metres to one of those anyway.

Before I left the shores of Antarctica for the last time, I made one tiny adjustment to one of the promises we had been asked to honour. I headed towards a steep bank of unblemished fresh snow, leaving only my footprints as we had been instructed, but then leant forward and, with the index finger of my gloved right hand, I drew the number seven into the snow. It was time to say goodbye to my seventh continent.

Our zodiac didn't take us directly back to the ship. Steering through the brash ice, we took one final tour around this incomparable and utterly jaw-dropping landscape. A lone Weddell seal snoozing on his iceberg home, towering glacier walls, layers of snow at the surface like the rings of a tree trunk, their depth demarcating the severity of successive winters and menacing caves at water level that nobody would ever want to venture close to. Long may Antarctica retain its unique beauty, and we all have a part to play in that in the way we live our lives.

* * * * *

As we ate our lunch back on board, the captain had already set sail for Ushuaia. It would not be the same smooth voyage as the outward journey; the Drake lake had become the Drake shake. We quickly learned the wide-leg stance as we queued for our meals; we grabbed at anything as we moved around the stairwells and corridors of the ship, and mealtimes became a whole new experience. The soup course disappeared from the lunch and dinner menus, as the soup simply refused to remain in the bowls. Mealtime drinks became a fond memory after bottles and glasses crashed to the floor as the ship pitched and rolled on the waves. Indeed, we would probably have joined them had the outer seat in each row not been bolted to the floor. It was a question of hanging on to your dinner plate and trying to eat your meal as quickly as possible before it attempted to escape your clutches. Not surprisingly, there were rather more empty spaces in the dining room at mealtimes as many struggled to cope with their nausea. To my own surprise, I was not one of them; the patches and wrist bands had proven to be a good strategy, for me at least.

There was plenty to keep us entertained on the return journey. The multimedia room on the ship held several computers on to which we could download our own personal photographs as well as take copies of photos from others; a wonderful way to make sure we all went home with a fantastic pictorial record of our epic adventure. We were also royally entertained with a succession of documentaries on early Antarctic explorers and their expeditions; Harry from One Ocean, a glaciologist, gave us a fascinating insight into Antarctic ice, and Karen, his wife, spoke of the role of women in Antarctica. And, as if we hadn't seen enough of penguins, we were treated to a showing of the animated movie *Happy Feet*, the story of a dancing penguin but incorporating some serious environmental messages as well.

As we came within first sight of Cape Horn and the South American continent, the ship slowed and the seas began to lose some of their ferocity. Even soup returned to the menu!

Liz from One Ocean had put together a slide and video show of our exploits, which we could all take away with us on a memory stick. There were few dry eyes in the room as we relived so many magical moments. A fundraising auction for some of the memorabilia from the trip raised a fantastic amount of money for Oceanites, a non-profit scientific organisation that monitors the effects of climate change and the impact of tourism on Antarctica. This was followed by the captain's dinner, a chance to give thanks to the Russian crew, the One Ocean staff, the Marathon Tours team and, of course, each other for a trip none of us would ever forget. Afterwards, we each ate a slice of a massive celebration cake, adorned with iced zodiacs, kayaks, icebergs, whales, penguins and seals and, would you believe, the evening ended with just one more party in the bar.

When Sinckers made his final wake-up call the following morning, we were docked in Ushuaia and Maxwell had been released back to his natural habitat. Sadly in some ways, we were back in the land of the internet. As much as it brings to our lives, we all survived without it for ten days and we were a much tighter community as a result of having talked to each other rather than being constantly distracted by messages from afar. With a little bit of time before our flight onwards to Buenos Aires, a few of us found the coffee bar, with wifi, that we had used on our way out. My phone exploded with notifications.

We flew as a group back to the domestic airport in the capital. From there, some were transferring to the international airport for their flights back home. Others, including myself, had one more night in Buenos Aires before returning home the following day. It was time for some fond farewells but, as is the case on these occasions, in the hope that one day we would meet up again, perhaps at another crazy event. This is where the internet does comes into its own. We may live our lives in various places dotted around the planet but retaining contact with great running friends is so much easier these days.

* * * * *

As I sat in my taxi on my way to the airport the following day, my phone rang. It was a lady from Halesowen University of the Third Age (U3A) in the UK.

'I understand you have been running in Antarctica. Can you come and give us a talk about it?'

Oh, please let me get home first!

* * * * *

It was indeed a very warm homecoming, with plenty of media interest in my story. Just a couple of days after returning, Chris and I had been invited into the BBC Radio Shropshire studios to have an on-air chat with their breakfast time host. We had expected maybe five minutes of airtime, with Chris talking about his involvement with parkrun and his charity event, Dark Run, and me talking about the seven continents achievement, but we took up almost a full half hour of the show, such was the presenter's interest in our stories.

Invitations to give illustrated talks on my trip began to follow that initial one from Halesowen U3A. Perhaps the most intriguing as a venue was an open prison close to where I lived, where I gave a talk to around 100 invited guests, with around 40 of the inmates joining the audience. The prison, Hewell Grange, was housed inside a magnificent country mansion, the former home of the Earl of Plymouth, with gardens designed by Capability Brown and sprawling grounds, including its own lake. Afterwards, I held some very engaging conversations with several of the inmates, who seemed genuinely inspired by my tales, and it would be nice to think that it might help at least one of them to avoid making the same mistakes in the future that put them in there in the first place.

Then there were invitations to talk at schools, with children as young as four in the audience. A very different type of talk naturally but nevertheless, in an age where childhood obesity is becoming such a problem, an opportunity to inspire them to lead healthier and more active lifestyles, as well as to get a few environmental messages across. Those two humpback whales had really hardened my attitude to the ways we deal with our plastic waste in particular.

And then, of course, came the big day, my 70th birthday celebrations. In fact, they lasted about a week, with the actual day falling on a Tuesday, with a surprise party being held the following weekend. I had an inkling that something was taking place, as I had been asked previously if I would be free on that day and did have a say in who to invite. However, the form of the celebrations was largely a conspiracy between Chris and my running friend, Phillipa, with secret Facebook groups keeping me out of the loop. It was a fabulous evening, surrounded by friends and family, many of whom had travelled some distance to be there. It was particularly nice to see Jon again, the man who had successfully guided Miles, my blind running friend, across 140 miles of the Sahara Desert. Sadly, Miles himself couldn't make it. There was laughter as my brother, Dave, read excruciating passages from one of our old camping logbooks, destroying my 'never give up' credibility in one fell swoop, and an emotional moment for me when Chris presented me with a photobook in which numerous friends and family had shared a photograph of us together and written a few words to recall some of our interactions. It was very humbling to read it.

I even tried my hand at Irish dancing, which is usually well out of my comfort zone. I am proud to say that, through careful pacing, I was last man standing with a glass of beer in my hand at the end of what had been a very long evening.

* * * * *

So that's it, then? I've passed the age of 70 and completed my ambition of running at least a half marathon on all seven continents. Is it time to retire my running shoes and put my feet up? I guess you know by now that's not me.

It is over six years since I ran my last full marathon, and that was in Rome. I will be honest; these days I much prefer the half marathon distance as I know I can complete it without too much pain and discomfort, and that I will recover quickly afterwards. After all, my main motivation for running now is enjoyment rather than being driven by the stopwatch. Having said that, the full 26-mile, 385 yards marathon distance, commemorating the legendary run of Pheidippides, retains a unique status amongst distance running enthusiasts. I have always said that I will attempt one more marathon once I have moved into decade number eight and, for that, I will return to Italy with Chris and hopefully run the Venice marathon later this year.

There are other targets as well. The circumference of our planet at the equator has been measured as 24,902 miles. Currently, my running log has me some 4,700 miles short of that. Now that would be a nice goal to achieve; maybe another three to four years at my current rate.

And then there is parkrun. I cannot understate the difference that parkrun has made to my life: a whole new circle of friends who you know will be there for you when life gets a little tough sometimes. For someone who has focused on long-distance races throughout his running journey, a weekly five-kilometre run might not seem that relevant. But parkrun is so much more than just five kilometres. It is about the range of abilities that are welcome, the camaraderie, the community spirit amongst participants and volunteers. Seeing people willing to push their bodies a little beyond their comfort zone in order to become better versions of themselves. Watching people's faces when they achieve what they never thought possible. It literally changes people's lives.

I was 64 years old when I completed my first parkrun. Saturday mornings used to begin with a bit of a hangover after over-celebrating the end of the working week. Now, those five kilometres, first thing on a Saturday morning, set me up for the whole weekend. I sometimes reflect on how I could have performed had parkrun been around earlier in my running career. At my best, I might have been able to break that magic

20-minute barrier. These days, I could only do that with the aid of a petrol combustion engine. Earlier this year, I made it to the magic 250 parkruns milestone and can now wear the coveted green T-shirt. Can I make it to 500? I don't see why not and I will give it my best shot.

Now that I have completed all seven of the continents, should I stop travelling the world? I think not. After Venice, I already have my eye on a race on Easter Island, another opportunity to meet again with past running friends from around the globe and make some new ones, too.

I know it can't go on for ever, but this particular grandfather is not throwing in the towel just yet.